Let My People Go

Let My People Go

Insights to Passover and the Haggadah

Jeffrey M. Cohen

JASON ARONSON INC.
Northvale, New Jersey
Jerusalem

This book was set in 12 pt. Palatino by Alabama Book Composition

Library of Congress Cataloging-in-Publication Data

Cohen, Jeffrey M.
    Let My People Go: Pesach and Haggadah Insights / by Jeffrey M. Cohen.
        p. cm.
    ISBN 0-7657-6204-8
    1. Passover. 2. Haggadah. I. Title.

BM695.P3 C64 2002
296.4'37—dc21

                                                                    2001035525

Printed in the United States of America on acid-free paper. For information and catalog, write to Jason Aronson Inc., 230 Livingston Street, Northvale, NJ 07647-1726, or visit our website: www.aronson.com

To Gloria
with affection and gratitude

And to our children,
Harvey and Lorraine,
Suzanne and Keith,
Judith and Bob,
Lewis and Suzanne

And to our adored grandchildren,
Joel, Phil, Alex, Elliot, Abigail,
Ariel, Charlotte, Madeleine,
Sasha and Zack.

Contents

CONTENTS

Preface

The festival of Pesach excites most Jews, but none more than the younger generation for whom it is invested with its own unique appeal and an emotional relevance that no other festival can match. Family celebrations have a special magical spirit for children, and Pesach, and the Seder in particular, is a family celebration par excellence.

But it goes deeper than that. Children respond instinctively to this festival because they sense that it speaks directly to their hearts. They understand, and take pride in the fact, that Pesach personifies the child-hood stage of national development that their ancestors were at when they were called upon to celebrate the festival for the first time in ancient Egypt. And this is what the prophet Hoseah had in mind when he said: "For Israel was a child, and I loved him; and from Egypt I called out to my son" (11:1).

It is not surprising, therefore, that this is such a child-oriented festival, beginning with the fourfold biblical reference to children's expressed curiosity regarding the meaning of its rituals, a curiosity that is not expected in the context of any of the other biblical holy days. And it is that wide-eyed curiosity, that readiness to leap onto the time machine of biblical tradition and to alight at the very center stage of our ancient existential drama, that inspired another prophet to characterize the Messianic age in terms of "a restoration of the heart of children to their parents" (*Malachi* 3:24). Adults soon lose the capability for spiritual excitement and unbounded curiosity. And the spirit of the past and future redemption thus coalesce in the context of Pesach's objective, namely to restore that childlike excitement and curiosity to the heart of the adult community of Israel.

Perhaps this is why, having already written one lengthy book on the subject of this festival (*1001 Questions and Answers on Pesach* [Jason Aronson Inc., 1996]), I am drawn back to it once again. It speaks to the child within me; it challenges me to focus on the heaven-directed redemption of my people over three thousand years ago, and to marvel at the fact that my generation was the one privileged to witness the restoration of Jewish sovereignty in 1948, and to share the birth pangs, the promise, and the idealistic dreams of that cataclysmic period.

I am drawn back to our biblical and rabbinic sources in order to attempt to make sense of the oppression we have suffered, not only in ancient Egypt but in every subsequent age, as well as to understand the meaning and contemporary implications of freedom, and why we Jews, who would know its value more than any other nation, just cannot seem to exploit our newfound freedom in Israel for the cementing of internal cohesion and unity of purpose. The modern-day parallel with the redeemed generation of Israelites, who, notwithstanding "having seen the great hand of God," yet proved ungrateful, rebellious, and factious, is inescapable.

History certainly repeats itself. And if we do not learn from history, perhaps it is because we do not learn history! If we studied it closely, we might stand a chance of avoiding at least some of the many pitfalls that recur with monotonous and tragic regularity in every generation. If we explored our ancient sources, we might create a sense of perspective and regain that sense of unity and purpose that seems so woefully lacking among successive generations of political and religious leaders of our people.

This book is the distillation of my lectures, sermons, and articles on the subject of the background of the festival, the symbolism of its rituals, its philosophy, and its contemporary relevance and resonance. It is not only my training in the analytical approach, but also the child within me, that has allowed my imagination much scope in seeking out what I believe to be original interpretations of the familiar and central texts relating to this festival. As the Talmud and Midrash have been the repository for the preservation of ancient traditions, affecting the way we view and are inspired by our biblical history, and the way we are enabled to capture the authentic spirit of our festivals, it will be readily appreciated why I have made the Haggadah—the midrashic handbook of Pesach—the primary focus of my enquiry.

I am not alone, I know, in seeking to fathom precisely what the Haggadah is attempting to convey in any given passage. That exercise is, after all, the very essense of the mitzvah of *sippur yetzi'at mitzrayim*, the relating of the story of the Exodus, on Passover eve. The truth is, however, that, surprising as it may seem, on that eve we do not look at the original text and primary source—the biblical book of Exodus—to fulfill that duty, but rather at the *Haggadah shel Pesach*, a secondary, basically midrashic, source, passages of which (according to some scholars) date from as early as the third century B.C.E., but the majority of which emanates from centuries later.

Though the unbroken spell of the Haggadah may constitute a dilemma for those progressive ideologies that reject the authority of the talmudic/midrashic sages, their *halachah*, and oral traditions, for Orthodoxy, on the other hand, there is no dichotomy between oral tradition and written text. The former is a subfile of the latter, revealing supplementary information that, in the interest of conciseness and to facilitate the commitment of holy writ to memory, was not originally set down as a literary document, but passed down through the ages in oral form. And it is from this standpoint that I embody within this book expositions of both of those conjoint sources of this festival.

The Pesach Haggadah is a multiseamed mine of truly profound, stimulating, and soul-stirring concepts that speak to the heart and address the concerns and the theological, national, and moral dilemmas of our modern generation as vividly as they did to the generation to which they were first addressed. It is my hope that my readers will find the interpretations and insights that I have mined from those sources interesting, enlightening, and edifying.

I should like to express my thanks to the editors of the London *Jewish Chronicle* and the Jerusalem *Jewish Bible Quarterly* for permission to reprint articles, as well as to my main source of encouragement and inspiration, my dear wife, Gloria. I also thank Rabbi Professor Abner Weiss, the principal of the London School of Jewish Studies, for gracing this book with his illuminating Foreword, and my friend, Mr. Clive Boxer for reading the proofs.

Foreword

by Rabbi Abner Weiss

I first met Dr. Jeffrey Cohen in Beverly Hills, California. I was Senior Rabbi at Beth Jacob Congregation, the largest Orthodox community in the Western United States. Beth Jacob prided itself on selecting the most outstanding and articulate contemporary Jewish thinkers and writers for its Scholar-in-Residence programmes.

Dr. Cohen was the only scholar whom I had not met before extending him an invitation. So many people, however, spoke highly of his special gifts of mind and heart, that I was persuaded to bring him to the West Coast sight-unseen. We were not disappointed.

Although Dr. Cohen arrived sight-unseen, he was hardly an unknown figure in the world of Jewish scholarship. He is the celebrated author of an impressive array of publications, both scholarly and popular. His writing is lucid, his reasoning tight, and his ability to communicate with his reader enviable.

Most of Dr. Cohen's books relate to Jewish Liturgy and the Festival calendar. His latest offering belongs to both genres. It is both an in-depth exploration of the contemporary significance of Passover, and a sensitive exploration of the haggadah of Pesach, its liturgical centre piece.

To be sure, there are probably more editions of the Haggadah, with more commentaries of more variety than any other Jewish text. The great halachic masters have left their particular imprint on this most loved little book. The Hasidic giants have embellished its text with their own insights. There are liberation haggadot, feminist haggadot, and, now, templates for do-it-yourself haggadot for the personal computer. One wonders how much is left to be said about this text.

Dr. Cohen's book is an indication that a great deal has been left unsaid by his predecessors. But this is not a commentary on the haggadah. Dr. Cohen has already done that. It is a compilation of the central ideas and problematica suggested both by the haggadah and by other aspects of the Passover festival.

Dr. Cohen ranges wide in his analyses. He does not shy away from dealing with the Theodocy. Eschewing the theology of self blame and guilt, he makes reference to Salman Rushdie's experiences to illustrate his view that suffering can produce growth. He articulates the perplexing existential problem of "the difficult freedom" with disarming simplicity. He invokes self-psychology in seeking an understanding of the re-experiencing of Egyptian slavery and liberation, and emphasizes that the central imperative of the Exodus is to ethical sensitivity and moral activism.

Dr. Cohen is not afraid of being controversial. He unabashedly takes issue with the Sages of the Talmud and Midrash. Even the great Maimonides and Nachmanides do not escape his critical analysis. Few Orthodox rabbis would dare to suggest such startlingly different explanations of the paschal lamb ceremony—and carry it off with such brilliance.

Dr. Cohen is always original. Some of his insights and interpretations are breath-taking. His suggestion, for example, that the four sons represent different stages of individual spiritual growth and development is strikingly new, and psychologically very sound. His discussion of spiritual intimacy and covenantal election in the context of the Dayyenu hymn is masterly.

Dr. Cohen makes his readers conscious that, though many things change, they essentially remain the same. The chapters which uncover the Judaeo-Christian polemic embedded in the Seder ritual are particularly illuminating. His citations of christological interpretations of the haggadah by the contemporary 'Jews for Jesus' groups proves his point both dramatically and simply.

I was deeply moved by Dr. Cohen's discussion of love and marriage. His call for spontaneity, discovery and love is well taken. His objections to parental and societal intrusiveness need to be heard.

I am privileged to have been invited to write this Foreword. Since coming to live in England to direct the academic programmes of the London School of Jewish Studies, I have had many occasions to meet and converse with Dr. Jeffrey Cohen. He is certainly one of the most gifted members of the Anglo-Jewish Rabbinate. I am honoured to have him as a friend and colleague.

1

꒳

The Fertility of the
Early Israelites

The book of Exodus opens with a statement of the unprecedented growth rate of the Jewish people in Egypt: "And the Children of Israel were fruitful and increased abundantly, and multiplied, and waxed exceeding mighty, and the land was filled with them" (Exodus 1:7). This theme is taken up in the *Tzei ul'mad* passage of the Passover Haggadah, which quotes a corroborative verse from Deuteronomy 26:5: "The Syrian (Laban) attempted to destroy my father (Jacob), so he went down to Egypt and settled there. Though few in number, he soon became a nation that was great, mighty and populous *(varav)*."

The Haggadah then proceeds to clarify the latter word *(varav)*, linking it to the more emphatic and feminine form, *revavah*, as used by the prophet Ezekiel in his graphic metaphor for the rapidity with which Israel grew and developed in Egypt, as akin to that of a young girl attaining her puberty. As the latter stage presages a readiness for marriage, so Israel's rapid growth into a nation was an essential part of the divine plan that Israel should be ready to become the beloved of God as soon as she leaves Egypt: "I caused you to increase *(revavah)*, like the growth of the field. You thrived, grew up and came to full puberty . . ." (Ezekiel 16:7).

It has challenged the wit of commentators, ancient and modern, to provide an adequate explanation of this fecundity, dramatic enough in its proportions as to make the new Pharaoh conclude that *"the people of the children of Israel are too numerous and too mighty for us"* (v. 9).

Nahum M. Sarna seemingly evades the problem. On verse 7, his only observation is that

> *this description of the extraordinary fertility of the Israelite population carries strong verbal echoes of the divine blessings of fertility bestowed upon humankind at Creation and after the Flood. It suggests a conception of the community of Israel in Egypt as a microcosm, a miniature universe, self-contained and apart from the larger Egyptian society—the nucleus, spiritually speaking, of a new humanity.*[1]

He makes no attempt, however, to deal with the practical issue raised by the verse, namely how to account for the birthrate. He similarly evades the issue in his

2

comment on verse 9, though he utilizes the opportunity there to deal with the Hyksos invasion, as if suggesting that this was the implication of the rapid population increase. The verse does not say, however, that the Israelite presence was "swelled" by the arrival of any (Semitic) newcomers. It affirms unequivocally that the indigenous Israelites were *themselves* fruitful and prolific.

Samuel David Luzzatto (1800–1865) quotes, and disposes of rather disdainfully, the views of the distinguished German theologian, Johann David Michaelis, who appears to have been one of the earliest "modern" scholars to have addressed the problem. In the context of Michaelis' treatment of the verse, "about six hundred thousand men on foot, besides children" (Exodus 12:37) left Egypt, Luzzatto observes that:

> *this suggests that at least two million people left Egypt. But this defies normal human increase that, in the course of only 400 years, such a large nation could evolve. Now, Johann David Michaelis has attempted to rationalize this in several ways. First, that Middle Eastern men married when they are about thirteen to fifteen. But this is rubbish, for, truly, marrying so young has the effect of weakening the body and reducing its procreative power (!). Secondly, he asserts that Israelite men married more than one wife. This is also rubbish, for if one man married several women, or even just two, then it would simply have the effect of leaving many other men without wives, since the number of males and females is fairly uniform. He further explains that*

3

Israelite men had a longer life span, living to a hundred years and more. This is also rubbish, since the psalmist says that "the days of our years are three score years and ten" (Psalm 4:10).

Now our sages have suggested that they bore six at one time, a tradition corroborated by ancient writers who affirmed that the Nile waters increased fertility, to the extent that Egyptian women generally bore twins (see Aristotle, Pliny, Seneca). It could also be that the circumcision had that effect on the birthrate, as Philo suggested in his commentary . . .

It was, in fact, the blessing of God and His providence that preserved the Hebrews from falling victim to illnesses that killed other babies, in order to fulfil His promise to Abraham (Genesis 15:13) that, at the end of 400 years, they would become a nation which could exist and prosper in the land of its inheritance.[2]

In considering Israelite fertility, it is vital, however, not to overlook the fact that the Torah credits that unnatural increase as having reached unprecedented proportions already in the very earliest period of their sojourn in Egypt (see Exodus 1:7). It is challenging, therefore, to see if we can explain that phenomenon in terms of our present demographic knowledge.

From studies of the demography of ethnic minorities under repressive regimes, as well as from our own observation of the high birthrate of free refugee minorities, particularly in the first few generations, before they become acculturated, we know that they instinctively compensate for their physical and economic powerlessness by building up their internal human resources, seeking refuge and solace in the security of offspring and family. Numerical strength gives the illusion of power, whether or not one is creating mere cannon fodder.

Critics have consistently doubted the biblical record of such a dramatic increase in the Israelite birth rate, or that, from the seventy souls of the family of Jacob who came down to Egypt, such a vast nation could have been created within a mere one hundred years. The popular, 'scholarly' explanation is that the Israelites had been part of the Semitic Hyksos force that invaded and occupied the throne of Egypt in 1730 B.C.E. An influx of their Israelite brethren followed the victorious army and settled in Egypt, which, as the primary center of culture, prosperity and opportunity, offered much greater security and stability than the regularly drought-stricken lands of Canaan and Syria. This alone may explain how Joseph—a fellow Semite—could have risen to the highest office in the state. It also explains how the Israelite numbers could have swelled so dramatically, to the extent that they were deemed a threat to the state by such Pharaohs as Ramesses II, a successor of the liberator of Egypt, Ahmose I, who banished the hated Hyksos in 1570 B.C.E. According to this reconstruction of events, it was not natural increase, but successive waves of immigration into Egypt by fellow Semites, that accounted for the unprecedented Israelite growth.

This neat identification with the Hyksos has its historical and archaeological problems, however, as does the identification of the Hebrews with the Hapiru or Habiru, mentioned in contemporary Akkadian records. The question we would address, therefore, is whether there is any other way of rationalising that unique level of Israelite fertility. We believe that some demographic statistics about the growth rate of the Jewish people during the 19th century may be pertinent to this question.

At the dawn of that century, the Jewish population of Europe numbered some two million. By the beginning of the 1880s this had grown, by natural increase, to nearly seven million, with a Jewish rate of increase that was twice as fast as that of the gentile population. H.H. Ben-Sasson lists several factors to account for this "demographic miracle," notable among which was the improved sanitary conditions during this period, which banished hereditary causes of disease, epidemic, death, and infant mortality by new and effective methods of garbage and sewage disposal and provision of fresh water.

Now, while the gentile population also enjoyed such benefits, and while there was no significant difference between the Jewish and gentile birthrates, yet that phenomenal Jewish increase was brought about by their much higher-than-average life span, caused by a very low infant and adult mortality rate, which that writer attributes to "the specific character of Jewish society, with its religious and cultural traditions." He defines these to include, primarily, the unique Jewish devotion and care of their sick, as well as:

> *the greater stability of the family . . . . the infrequency of venereal diseases, the higher status of the woman*

within the family, the care lavished on babies and small children, abstinence from alcohol, the readiness of the individual and the community to undergo considerable economic sacrifice in order to help others, and the lengthy tradition of charitable deeds.[3]

In the light of such considerations, and given the prosperous conditions under which the families of Jacob lived in the early period of their sojourn in Egypt, we suggest that it is not inconceivable that their demographic increase might well have been in accordance with the dramatic proportions described in Exodus Chapter 1.

Now, we have, in fact, outlined two diametrically opposite scenarios that could account for such growth: repression, creating a situation of ethnic withdrawal from the host society, or, on the other side of the scale, freedom and prosperity, bringing with it a dramatic improvement in standard of living, with a consequently healthy diet, relaxation, sanitary conditions, and care.

We suggest that the combination of both of these conditions, at different periods during the sojourn in Egypt, might have been responsible for driving up the Israelite birthrate. In the early-Joseph period and its aftermath, it was the good life in Goshen, where they enjoyed the *meitav ha'aretz*, "the very best conditions that the land had to offer" (Genesis 47:6, 11). They were "sustained" by Joseph, at a time when "there was no bread throughout the rest of the land" (vv. 12–13). So, the Israelites thrived physically, and the women were healthy and strong, to the extent that their midwives could offer a plausible excuse to Pharaoh as to why they were not destroying the Hebrew male children at birth. They told him that, "the Hebrew women are not like the [sickly] Egyptian women, for they are 'lively' *(kiy chayyot heinah)*," that is, blooming with health and vitality.

By contrast, the Egyptian population was undernourished and sickly, with the famine taking a high toll on mortality (see v. 19: *Lamah namus le'einekha, gam anachnu gam admateinu,* "Why shall we perish before your eyes, both us and our land?"), and with the undernourished pregnant Egyptians miscarrying and finding the act of giving birth both painful and protracted.

And in the later period, when the "new king" introduced extensive measures to enslave the Hebrews and make their conditions of life and work intolerable, this very opposite situation could very likely have had the identical effect of sustaining an increase in the Israelite birthrate, to the extent that the rabbis, perhaps with a touch of exaggeration, speak of "sextuplets arriving at each birth."[4]

It is not difficult, therefore, to understand Pharaoh's great fear of the Israelites and his assertion that they were "more numerous and strong" than the indigenous population. The latter was being decimated by starvation and disease, while the Israelite percentage of the overall population was increasing dramatically, both in relation to the Egyptian losses as well as by their own increased fertility.

NOTES

1. Nahum M. Sarna, ed., The JPS Torah Commentary, (Philadelphia, New York, Jerusalem: The Jewish Publication Society, 1991), p. 4.

2. S. D. Luzzatto, *Peirush SHaDaL al Chamishah Chumshei Torah* (Tel Aviv, Dvir, 1965), p. 256.

3. H. H. Ben-Sasson, ed., *A History of the Jewish People* (Cambridge, Mass: Harvard University Press, 1976), p. 790.

4. *Midrash Shemot Rabba* 1:7. Other traditions (*ad loc.*) speak hyperbolically of twelve, or even sixty, being born at a time, clearly reflecting the attempt of different sages to express the uniqueness of the demographic development at that period.

2

ক্ক

Why We Were Slaves
in Egypt

I.

Pesach celebrates our emergence from slavery to freedom at the dawn of our history. But why we had to go into slavery in the first place is something of a mystery. After all, what grievous crime had the descendants of Abraham perpetrated that they should have deserved such a harsh punishment? Later on in Israelite and Jewish history there are any number of collective sins and rebellions that might have justified such a punishment. But at that stage of Israel's pre-history, it is difficult to imagine anything that could have justified the Egyptian bondage.

Commentators allow their imagination free rein to try and explain it. Abravanel quotes Rabbeinu Nissim

Gaon to the effect that, when God first disclosed to Abraham that his offspring would suffer affliction for four hundred years in an alien land (Genesis 15:13), this was not by way of a pre-ordained divine punishment for any specific sins of the forefathers, but simply a revelation of what would occur as a direct result of Israelite sin while *in* Egypt. Had it not been for that sin (probably of idolatry), their sojourn would have been much shorter and less painful.[1]

Other commentators do view God's disclosure, however, as a punishment for patriarchal sin, the precise nature of which is withheld from us. For Moses Nachmanides, it lay in Abraham's deception of Pharaoh when he passed off his wife, Sarai, as his sister[2]. Abraham displayed a lack of faith in God's protective power, for which his offspring were deprived of that protection and exposed to the tyranny of Pharaoh. This is in conformity with the principle *Ma'asei avot siman l'banim*, "the action of the parents presage the fate of their offspring."

In a similar approach, the Talmud[3] also connects the bondage to a lack of faith on Abraham's part, specifically when God promised him that his offspring would one day possess the land of Canaan (Genesis 15:7), and Abraham replied, "But how will I know that I shall inherit it?" (v. 8).

Viewing the bondage as a divine visitation for a specific sin committed by Abraham directs us to a more obvious situation where he behaves with a hardness of heart, which stands out in stark contrast to the kindliness and generosity of spirit in which Abraham is otherwise portrayed in the Torah. We refer to his and Sarah's ill-treatment of their Egyptian handmaid, Hagar, leading, in Sarah's case, to indefensible physical abuse[4], which Abraham should never have countenanced.

The physical abuse suffered by Abraham's offspring in Egypt provides a telling counterpart to the abuse he and his wife inflicted upon that Egyptian girl; and the "hardness of heart" displayed by Pharaoh on so many occasions is also powerfully evocative of a similar hardness of heart on the part of Abraham and Sarah. Other commentators suggest that the Egyptian bondage was punishment for the kidnap, ill-treatment, and sale of Joseph by his brothers. Just as Joseph was sold into Egypt, so the tribes of Israel were enslaved there, to learn the lesson of living in peace with their brethren, a lesson that was essential if they were ever going to merge into a unified nation, in a land of their own, bound together by cords of brotherhood and collective identity.

Another view that is far more charitable to the Patriarchs, and does not focus upon any crime, sin, or misdemeanor at the dawn of our history, has it that the Egyptian slavery was a necessary training period, to toughen Israel physically for the many confrontations and battles they would have to endure while traveling through the desert and while attempting to conquer the Holy Land and banish the war-like tribes that inhabited it, in order to settle in their place. In other words, the Egyptian experience was for Israel's ultimate benefit, although they could never have been expected to appreciate it at the time.

This approach may be extended to understand the enslavement as a necessary *spiritual* training period. This may be illustrated with reference to the famous Booker Prize-winning author, Salman Rushdie, whose book, *Satanic Verses*, written in 1988, offended Muslims so much that they issued a *fatwa*, banning his book. This was accompanied by a call to Muslims to assassinate him for his blasphemy, with a reward on his head of some four million dollars. To escape such a fate, Rushdie spent ten years in hiding, with two armed bodyguards to protect him at all times. He only emerged on rare occasions, to give an important lecture, attend a literary gathering, or to launch one of his books.

Now, a review of the first book that Rushdie wrote after the *fatwa* was lifted, contains an observation that is germane to our subject of the purpose of Israel's enslavement in Egypt.

The reviewer surveyed the many books that Rushdie had written since the appearance of his first in 1975, and including the most recent since the *fatwa* was lifted, and came to the conclusion that "oddly and impressively," the books Rushdie published during his time in hiding showed a marked upsurge of imaginative flair, creativity, and liveliness, which is absent from those that he wrote as a free man.[4]

This observation highlights a clearly positive aspect of restricted freedom. The molding of our people into a nation began in Egypt, with our rights curtailed and our freedom of movement denied. The only place where we were totally unfettered was in our unbounded creative imagination. Ironically, it was in the hostile environment of Egypt that the Israelites prepared the ground to become the most creative and educated nation of the ancient world, capable, but three months after leaving Egypt, of receiving a Torah and of absorbing the loftiest ideas and spiritual concepts.

Perhaps *that* was why they were sent into Egypt: So that they would have no other distractions, but could turn their physical restrictions to their best advantage, enabling them to develop and cultivate to the highest degree their creative, poetic, intellectual, and spiritual faculties.

II

One of the most remarkable statements contained in the Haggadah occurs early on, amid the historical survey of early Israelite history: *Mitchilah ovdei avodah zara* (other versions: *kokhavim) hayu avoteinu,* "Our ancestors started out as idolaters, but now God has brought them near to his service."

It is remarkable because it contradicts every first and basic principle to which the ancients were committed in the literary and dramatic presentations of their national origins. That principle was the commitment to idealize, glamorize, and mythologize their national primogenitors.

Feelings of national security were engendered and enhanced by proclaiming the invincibility of the geographical gods who guided the destiny of any particular country or people. The identification of Roman emperors and ancient Near Eastern kings as gods served that identical purpose: to vest divine invincibility in the person of the one who symbolized the purest expression and epitome of the national spirit.

Figures of the gods in ancient Canaanite and Greek temples, and imperial statues throughout the Roman empire, served not only to glorify the deity and aggrandize the emperor, but, more importantly, to disseminate feelings of strength, confidence, and superiority among the people as a whole.

It is against this background that we have to view the incredibly contrasting statement in the Haggadah that our own national origins lie not in a situation of oneness with, but rather one of estrangement from, the God who called us into being! This sentiment goes entirely against the grain of all ancient nationalistic and religious propriety. Indeed, the Mishnah[5] insists that *Matchil b'ganut*, "the Haggadah must commence with a pejorative reference to Israel." This takes the form of the *Avadim Hayyinu* passage, declaring that "we began our national saga as slaves," and *Mitchilah ovdei avodah zara hayu avoteinu*, "Our earliest ancestors were idolaters."

The Jew is thus conditioned never to idealize himself, but to acknowledge at all times his lowly origins and spiritual waywardness, and to be guided by those considerations when developing his philosophy of life, to the extent that he will feel an instinctive sense of kinship and empathy with all those who suffer hardship and discrimination for similar reasons.

In truth, we Jews have generally been bitterly self-critical. Perhaps that is one of the keys to our survival. We have always sought to discover the reasons why life and history yield the results they do, and we have never been lulled into a fatalistic stance. As a nation of philosophers, we have striven to be master analysts of our fate, believing, albeit naively, that by so doing we would be able to anticipate hostility and forestall it.

Those two tendencies—to be self-critical and to forever attempt to analyze the reasons why events, especially tragic ones, occur—underlie a quite amazing Talmudic explanation of why Abraham was punished that his seed should be subservient to the Egyptians for two hundred and ten years:

> *Rabbi Abbahu said in the name of Rabbi Eleazar: It was because of the sin of Abraham in having drafted students of the Torah (identified by* Rashi *with the young converts he had made in Haran[6]) into battle, as it states, "And he mustered his trained men, those (spiritually) reared in his house" (Gen. 14:14). Samuel said: It was because he presumed to put the reliability of God's promise that he would inherit the land to the test, when he queried: "How will I know that I shall possess it?" (Gen. 15:8). Rabbi Yochanan said: It was on account of his having surrendered up (to the idolatrous king of Sodom) potential converts to religion, as it is written, [And the king of Sodom said to Abraham,] "Give me the people (i.e., the captives rescued by Abraham in battle) and you keep the booty for yourself" (Gen. 14:21).[7]*

Students of Midrash and Talmudic history will undoubtedly attempt to pinpoint the rationale of each of the three "sins" that our father, Abraham, is charged with perpetrating, and which clearly reflect the political tensions and issues with which those three scholars of the early Talmudic period grappled, rather than to view them as reflecting any real situation in the life of Abraham. After all, we could hardly credit those great talmudists and profound thinkers with seriously espousing a theology that would justify the oppression and enslavement of an entire nation for more than two centuries merely as punishment for a single act of either omission or commission on the part of an early ancestor.

The reference in the second of the Ten Commandments to God "visiting the sins of the fathers upon the children, upon the third and fourth generations, to them that hate me," constitutes no objection here, since that threat is mentioned specifically in the case of the practice of idolatry. Furthermore, the key phrase, "to them that hate me," is universally interpreted (following *Targum Onkelos*) to refer only to a situation wherein each of those generations continues the iniquity of their parents' generation, a situation that could hardly be related to any of the above-quoted "sins" of father Abraham! Again, Deuteronomic law makes it quite clear that, "Fathers shall not be put to death for children, neither shall children be put to death for fathers; every man shall die for his own sin" (Deut. 24:17).

So we can only understand the above Talmudic passage as a piece of polemical exposition, wherein the key factor, for Rabbi Abbahu at least, was the burning contemporary issue of drafting students of the yeshivot (Talmudic academies) into the army. Since, in Roman times, there was no official Jewish army, we may conjecture that the reference is to participation in any of the periodic Jewish insurrections against Rome. Rabbi Abbahu sought to bolster his vehement opposition to such a draft by postulating the Egyptian enslavement as a punishment for father Abraham's encouragement of this practice.

The issue of drafting religious students into the modern Israeli army, which causes such a division between members of the *hesder yeshivot* and those on the extreme right of the religious spectrum, was clearly also an issue in religious circles of the first few centuries. The great Rabbi Akivah, who acted as armour-bearer for Bar-Kochba in his heroic rebellion against the Roman occupation, would clearly have rejected outright Rabbi Abbahu's identification of the "sin" of Abraham.

The second explanation of the Egyptian enslavement, suggested by the sage Samuel, which attributes it to Abraham's "sin" in having sought proof from God that he would truly inherit the land, may be explained against the background of Samuel's fame as an outstanding astronomer. The popular astrological belief had it that one's fate was determined by the position of the stars, and that man was hopeless to alter what was predetermined. Samuel objected vehemently to such a view, and he taught that man's fate was in his own hands, and that, as a reward for good deeds, his fate could be changed for good.

Samuel's suggestion of Abraham's "sin" was in line with his view in this respect. It was not appropriate, he wished to stress, to ask God to provide categorical proof for any future reality, since that reality was not cast in stone, and might be altered, for better or worse, depending upon the deeds of the person or nation concerned. Samuel was clearly using the issue of Abraham and that of the rationale of the Egyptian slavery in order to attack that popular astrological belief in augury.

The final suggestion, that of Rabbi Yochanan, that Abraham's "sin" was that of missing the opportunity to make converts of all the captive soldiers that he had rescued, is clearly a subtle piece of propaganda in the ongoing dispute regarding the benefit or otherwise to Judaism of accepting converts. Whereas there were those who believed that "converts are as unwelcome as a skin eruption,"[8] and that it was the converts among the Israelites who had been responsible for the making of the Golden Calf,[9] other sages went to the very opposite extreme, and there are numerous passages in rabbinic literature that wax lyrical about the dizzy spiritual heights to which true converts are elevated. An indication that the consensus was with the latter approach may be gauged from the fact that, in our central prayer, the *Amidah*, the *gerei hatzedek* (righteous converts) are listed in the blessing of *Al ha-tzaddikim* ("As for the righteous . . ."), which pays tribute to those who occupy the highest echelons of spiritual attainment.

We see then that the Talmud, though in this instance for the polemical reasons we have suggested, gives clear expression to the two tendencies to which we have referred: self-criticism (in this instance Abraham may be identified as the personification of the Jewish nation) and, secondly, the constant and curious analysis and desire for explanation of everything, especially the evil, that befell our people.

Thus, the *Mitchilah ovdei avodah zara* passage, which properly opens the Haggadah, and proclaims unashamedly that our ancestors began as idolaters, is offering its own rationale for the slavery in Egypt. It was not, as the Talmudic passage we have analyzed has it, the result of some failed religious opportunity on the part of Abraham, but rather a stage in the long and arduous process of national development and spiritual purging that began in the days of "Terach, father of Abraham and father of Nahor, who served other gods," and ended with God "keeping His promise to Israel *(Barukh shomer havtachato leYisrael)*." The "promise" also involved a lengthy slavery period that served the beneficial purpose of purging every trace of that propensity towards idolatry from the recesses of the Israelites' hearts.

Whereas, as we have seen, the Talmud explains the Egyptian bondage as a punishment for one individual's shortcoming, the Haggadah presents a far more mature analysis, viewing it as a constructive national exercise of self-purgation, providing the nation with a far more solid spiritual foundation from which to launch its future religious enterprises in the cause of becoming "a kingdom of priests and a holy nation."

NOTES

1. See commentary of Isaac Abravanel on Ex. 15:13.

2. See commentary of *Ramban* on Gen. 12:13.

3. Talmud *Nedarim* 32a.

4. The *Sunday Times* Books Section, 4 April 1999, p. 7.

5. *Pesachim* 10:4.

6. See *Rashi* on Gen. 12:5.

7. Talmud *Nedarim* 32a.

8. Talmud *Yevamot* 47a.

9. Midrash *Shemot Rabba*, Ch. 42.

CHAPTER

3

ૐ

Is Freedom a Jewish Concept?

Pesach focuses our minds each year on the nature of slavery and freedom, both in relation to the experiences of our ancestors in ancient Egypt as well as, subsequently, throughout our history.

The state of being free is one of the most precious and, at the same time, the most challenging. The achievement of freedom cannot be an ultimate objective and destination of itself. For it begs the question of "freedom to do what?" If one has nothing constructive with which to fill the vacuum left by enslavement, then the result will not be freedom but further repression. That was why God wasted no time in giving Israel the Torah, a mere seven weeks after they emerged into freedom.

There must have been a great temptation among the erstwhile Israelite slaves to throw off the yoke of discipline altogether. Many must have viewed official-dom of any kind—even the benign leadership of Moses and Aaron—as reminiscent of the "old order." Perhaps this attitude informed the rebellion of Korach, and his claim that "the entire congregation is holy, and the Lord is in their midst; why then do you exalt yourselves over the assembly of the Lord" (Numbers 16:3).

But that was a naïve and dangerous claim, because, as history has shown, without strong and wise leader-ship, the security and sovereignty of no nation or country is maintained. Without law and discipline, morality and responsibility, no people will thrive. But without belief in a higher Reality, to whom we are all accountable, then, indeed, Korach's argument would be justified, with the inevitable result that there would be a succession of power-crazed Korachs, leading coups, rebellions, and counterrebellions in order to seize the reins of power for personal vainglory, a situation with which the Third World is tragically familiar.

It is no different in our private lives, where total freedom is also a dangerous acquisition. Without disci-pline and moral restraint, without a strong sense that we are accountable for all our actions in relation to our fellow man, no relationships can grow, no mutuality of trust can be engendered; neither can families, schools, workplaces, or societies organize themselves.

In this respect, it is of great significance that, amid the entire biblical narrative covering the "call" of Moses, his mission to Pharaoh and the Exodus, nowhere is the word *freedom* specifically employed. Indeed, the use of several synonymous terms and circumlocutions make it appear as if there had been a conscious attempt to suppress that specific concept! Thus, there are references to Moses being told by God that He had come "to save His people from the hand of the Egyptians" (Exodus 3:8); to Moses being charged with "bringing forth the Children of Israel from Egypt" (v. 10); to God promising to bring them "to a land flowing with milk and honey" (v. 17); to Moses being instructed to tell Pharaoh, "Let [Israel] my son go, that he may serve Me" (v. 23); to Moses and Aaron telling Pharaoh, "Let my people go" (4:1); and to God reassuring Moses that "by a strong hand he shall let them go, and by a strong hand shall he drive them out of his land" (6:1). Yet, the word *chofshi*, employed over thirty times in the Bible to describe the attainment of a Hebrew slave's "freedom," is studiously avoided in all the passages dealing with the Exodus, where its use would have been so appropriate!

The Bible lexicons are unsure as to the primary meaning of the root *chafash*, which underlies that noun, *chofshi*. Indeed, there is only one example (Leviticus 19:20) of that root being used in a verbal form, *chupashah* ("freed"). We must conclude, therefore, that, although the notion of being "freed" *from* a situation of slavery was quite acceptable, yet the notion of being "free," of having total freedom, of becoming an uncontrolled, free spirit, was not.

Israel was not brought out of Egypt into *freedom*, but rather was the cruel and mindless Egyptian servitude replaced by the service of God.

To the Hebrew mind, freedom constitutes a vacuum, too easily filled by moral licence. It has to be replaced, therefore, by a commitment to a higher, more enriching and spiritual ideal. For that reason, a mere seven weeks after shedding the bonds of slavery, the Torah was given to Israel. They were clearly not yet intellectually and morally mature enough to fully comprehend or appreciate its meaning or the nature of the spiritual revolution inherent within it. But God could not afford to allow them any waiting period. The vacuum had to be filled. Their newfound freedom simply had to be anchored and pressed into a higher service.

The same applies to our modern-day redemption, in the form of the return of Jewry to its land. Too many Israelis view that "freedom" as the ultimate objective of the Jewish struggle over the past hundred years. It is, of course, a great and glorious achievement, but it is insufficient as a truly Jewish political philosophy. *Halakhah* (Jewish law) has to be accorded its place in the life of the State of Israel, and Judaism has to be shown to be relevant and enriching to the lives of all its citizens.

But it has to be *shown* to be capable of adapting to the needs and problems confronting a Jewry in a state of flux, a Jewry which has discovered and evolved alternative ways of expressing Jewishness, some of which have diluted or adapted halachic norms, and others which have totally rejected their authority. Orthodoxy is now in the ideological marketplace. It can choose to bury its head in the sand and pretend the competition does not exist, or it can develop a policy of inclusivism, and initiate a compassionate, tolerant and courageous campaign to solve such issues as conversion, *agunah*, and women's spirituality, making the real danger of losing one half of our people the justification for novel applications of the law.

But as long as Israeli society is divided up into ultra-Orthodox, Orthodox, Progressive, and secular camps, hermetically sealed off one from the other, the prospects of dialogue are remote. Without dialogue, there is no understanding of the tensions, influences, and dilemmas of the other, paving the way to suspicion, myth, delegitimization and even, God forbid, violence.

If Jewry is to survive, to fulfill the promise of redemption in its entirety, there has to be room around our nation's Seder table for every type of son, every level of commitment, and every variant ideology. We do not have to acknowledge the authenticity of their tradition, but we have to acknowledge them as fellow Jews struggling in the darkness for the light of God's presence. We have to apply to them the talmudic, *mimma nafshakh* ("whichever way you approach it") principle. This dictates that if we accept them as halachic Jews then we have to relate to them in the spirit of the biblical obligation of "love your neighbour as yourself." And if, on the other hand, we reject their Jewish halachic status, then we still have to observe Shammai's dictum: "And receive *all humankind* with a welcoming countenance" (*Pirkei Avot* 1:15).

If we can see our way to doing that, then we shall have some chance of achieving that great vision and challenge of our *Shabbat* afternoon liturgy: *Attah echad v'shimcha echad umiy k'amkha yisrael goy echad ba'aretz,* "You are One and Your Name is One, and who is like Your people, Israel, one people in their land?"

CHAPTER

4

ॐ

A Nation of Survivors!

I.

The Haggadah contains an enigmatic phrase, *Chayav adam lirot et atzmo ke'ilu hu yatza mimitzrayim*, "A man is duty bound to see himself as if he had personally gone forth out of Egypt." One would have thought that this was hardly something that could be legislated for as a "duty." It would surely depend on the power and vividness of the participants' imagination, on the depth of their historical consciousness, on their degree of emotional engagement with the texts they are reading and the rituals they are enacting, as well as the sense of realism that they are able to inject into their *Seder*. And not everyone is capable of achieving such high levels on all those counts, as to enable them to be authentically transported back in time, so as to feel that they, themselves, were truly living at the time, and experiencing the reality, of the Exodus.

We frequently hear of people who, under hypnosis, reveal successive layers of pre-existence. The sages had a similar notion that all the souls that were ever to be brought into being had already stood at the foot of Mount Sinai and accepted upon themselves the covenant of spiritual commitment for all future ages of Jewish history. The "duty" to regard ourselves as if we had personally come forth out of Egypt takes this notion just a little further back in time, to the day, some three months before Sinai, when "all Israel" came forth out of Egypt. That instruction is a call, therefore, for the impact of the Seder experience alone, without the artificial aid of hypnosis, to be sufficient to transport us back to a virtual reality.

But there are other ways of answering the problem of how it could be made obligatory for us to feel in any given way. It could, for example, be simply a call for us to focus on, and thereby recreate, one particular defining moment in the history of the Exodus.

Let us remind ourselves of the phraseology of that regulation: "A man is duty bound to see himself. . . ." We should have no difficulty whatsoever "seeing ourselves" as if we had personally left Egypt. This is because, as we go through life, we are accustomed to "seeing ourselves" and projecting ourselves in a host of different guises. We adopt numerous different personas to cope with, or forestall, strange or threatening situations, or to impress others. Sometimes we may adopt a macho image, on other occasions a vulnerable image. At times we may "see ourselves" as the oracles of wisdom, as having to step in and take the initiative, to save a situation, to be the leader. At other times we may view it as best policy to be passive, to keep our own counsel, to be among the led.

At different times of life, as a result of such things as peer attitudes or our own emotional state, we may "see ourselves" in differing lights. At times our mirror discloses to us a youthful-looking, confident person, able and ready to conquer the world. At other times we see ourselves as jaded and lacking in confidence. It is as if we are outside of ourselves, looking objectively and critically at another, unrelated person. We are truly conditioned to "seeing ourselves." It is not a difficult exercise.

Indeed, this ability to "see ourselves" is precisely what we mean by "liberation." The child's dawning awareness of his or her own self is referred to in psychology as "the mirror stage of life." Until the child is weaned, he or she experiences a total bonding with the mother, imagining itself as an extension of her body, part of her essence. The mirror stage is reached when the mother lifts the child to the mirror, and it suddenly discovers that it has an independent existence, that it has different physical and sexual characteristics, that it has an identity of its own, its own feelings, very strong, unbridled feelings, that make it aware of, and that demand some sort of relationship with, the mother, and, in consequence, the father. The parents can only fulfill their proper, and conjoint, roles in the emotional development of the child, and the child can only relate to, and come to terms with them both harmoniously, when he or she can "see himself," and define his own identity and situation in relation to them.

So the child is liberated, and becomes an independent person, only when it "sees itself" in relation to others, and against the backdrop of his environment. In the same way, on Seder night, we are told to enact the moment when our ancestors emerged from a situation when they experienced a slave-like and babe-like total dependency upon their Egyptian overlords, reliant on them for the bread they ate and the water they drank. *Chayav adam lirot et atzmo ke'ilu hu yatzah mimitzrayim,* "A man is obliged to 'see himself' as if he had personally come forth out of Egypt."

We are essentially being called upon to enact that mirror stage of development, that moment when the implication of exile suddenly dawned on our ancestors, and when, after a lengthy period of terrible apprehension, of unwillingness to follow Moses, of idealizing the cocoon of the known, albeit oppressive, present, out of the greater fear of the unknown future, they were suddenly able to "see themselves as if they had already escaped from Egypt." That was the climactic moment when they were ready to look into the mirror and see themselves as a potentially independent people, capable of self-determination and of assuming a separate and unique identity.

It is that fateful and decisive moment, the dawning of our ancestors' self-realization, that I suggest we are being asked to commemorate in those words, *Chayav adam lirot et atzmo . . . :* "A man should see himself as if he had emerged from *the dependency of* Egypt."

If there is a contemporary challenge in that rabbinic instruction, it is this: that we ask ourselves whether or not we have, indeed, personally emerged from the slavery that Egypt personified. Or are we still slaves? Slaves to an empty routine of life, to the exclusive and inexorable pursuit of wealth, to the dictates of those friends or associates who are taking us in the wrong moral direction? Slaves to our own addictions and passions? Slaves to the mores of a secular society? Slaves to a political system or social order that only free and courageous men can dare to challenge and change?

Our ancestors did all that. Our people have done it down the ages. *Chayav adam,* "A man is obliged . . ." to do it.

II.

A recent study by William B. Helmreich[1] refers to the unique contribution the survivors had made towards heightening Christian, as well as Jewish, awareness of the meaning of the Holocaust. The books and articles they had written, and the interviews and talks they had given to schools, students, and adults, had all contributed to a continued awareness of the meaning and significance of the Holocaust:

> *Every such encounter, every life touched, every con-*
> *science activated, represents a contribution made by the*

survivors towards ensuring that a Holocaust will not happen again. It is both their self-imposed duty and their opportunity to serve as the world's conscience as long as they are alive. And, to the degree that they succeed in this endeavor, they affect the course of history. . . . In as much as the survivors tend to see everything through the prism of their unique background, they influence society's thinking in other ways too.

At a World Gathering of Holocaust Survivors held in Jerusalem, oral histories were taped and deposited in Yad Vashem. One statement reads:

We live in a small world. We cannot afford to let anyone suffer. When the air is polluted, we all breathe it. . . . If the Jewish people, or any other people, are treated badly, we are all in for a bad time. If anything happens to one group of people, all the other minorities should stand up for them.

It is Helmreich's view that the impact those Holocaust survivors have had on others has been totally disproportionate to their numbers. Because of what they represent, because of the philosophy of despair they would have been expected to espouse, their affirmation of life, their hope, their optimism and faith in the human spirit, against all logic and in refutation of their own experience of a cruel reality, has had a profound effect on all whom they have encountered.

We Jews are, in essence, a survivor nation, formed from the loins of those who, by divine intervention, survived the "final solution" of an Egyptian pharaoh. His edict, that every Hebrew male child was to be drowned at birth, was handed down not only to the Hebrew midwives, but to every single Egyptian. Pharaoh's was the godless, megalomaniacal regime of a dictator who was incapable of discerning between right and wrong, justice and injustice. It was a regime that mocked at ethics, morals, human rights, and dignity.

That there were any "survivors" who remained immune to the effect of over two centuries of such moral pollution was a miracle in itself. That there was a nation of survivors that succeeded in preserving its sanity, as well as its faith, hope, sense of morality, concept of human dignity—ability to feel any emotion, let alone those of gratitude and joy sufficient to sing God's praises by the Red Sea—surpasses even the miraculous.

Perhaps that is why the theme of *zekher litziat mitzrayim*—"the remembrance of the Exodus from Egypt"—recurs with such regularity in our prayers and rituals. It is because the call to be a "survivor," to rise above even the worst human depravity, cannot be repeated often enough. With uncanny—many would say prophetic—foresight, the ancient sages who created our liturgy conditioned us for 2,000 years of "survival."

They challenged us to adopt the survivors' philosophy of refusing to be brutalized by brutality, but, quite the contrary, to emerge from it the victor rather than the vanquished, purged in spirit and ready to serve as a moral conscience for mankind. They conditioned us to become purveyors of sensitivity, compassion, and helpfulness to each and every minority that may need its soothing balm, and to become harbingers of hope, courage, and faith in the struggle for survival and existence.

Perhaps in this sense we may interpret those problematic words of the Haggadah: "And if God had not brought our forefathers out of Egypt, then we and our children and our children's children would have remained in servitude to Pharaoh in Egypt." This is another way of saying that, had we not been privileged to become "survivors" at the dawn of our history, and had that philosophy of resilience, self-reliance, faith, and optimism not been implanted within us, we could never have stepped through the fiery furnaces of Jewish history as courageously as we did. We could never have mustered the strength of mind, independence of spirit, confidence, and faith that we felt, preached, and inspired in every age, and which, at the same time, made us the focus and symbol of prejudice and persecution. We "would have remained in [mental] servitude," with a natural propensity to servility and national indolence.

Egypt taught us how to be survivors. In Egypt God gave us a mission to commit ourselves to the cause of all mankind's survivors. It is a mission that the Jewish state has zealously accepted, as witnessed by its aid programs and spontaneously extended humanitarian effort, frequently making it the first on the scene when any country is overwhelmed by natural or other disaster.

The concept of *zekher litziat mitzrayim*, remembering the Exodus from Egypt, may thus be seen, not as an obsession with our ancient past, but as constituting an eternal mandate to our people to work incessantly for the safety and *survival* of all God's threatened children, as expected of a nation of survivors.

NOTE

1. William B. Helmreich, "The impact of Holocaust survivors on American society: a socio-cultural portrait," *Judaism*, 39, no. 1 (Winter 1990): pp. 14–27.

5

৵৶

Searching for the *Chametz* and the Origin of Pesach

The very first of the mitzvot that we perform in preparation for the festival of Pesach is *Bedikat Chametz*, the search for the *chametz*. The blessing we recite over the search is a unique blessing. With all other blessings, there is a basic assumption that we are able to fulfill the rituals to which they relate in as complete and detailed a manner as required. However, as regards the blessing over the search for *chametz*, we are blessing a ritual that is virtually impossible properly to fulfill, for it is quite probable that, in the recesses of some dark corner or cupboard, there still lurks a speck of leaven, notwithstanding all our effort to clean the home meticulously. This was certainly the case in bygone ages before electric vacuum cleaners. Indeed, such a probability is admitted in the *Kol chamira* formula of *bittul* ("renunciation") that accompanies the blessing over the search. This petitions, specifically, that "all leaven . . . which I have not seen or removed, and the whereabouts of which I know not, may be annulled and regarded as ownerless as the dust of the earth." Why, then, did our tradition break with its convention and prescribe a blessing that embraces a negative element, namely, that which was overlooked, albeit inadvertently, from the focus of the mitzvah?

Appositely, one of the reasons given for not making a special blessing over the biblical mitzvah of relating the Exodus at the Seder is that it is too imprecise an exercise. The uneducated will restrict themselves to what they read in the Haggadah, if they can, indeed, read it in the original. Some may, indeed, glance at the translation, but there is no saying that they will alight upon a passage dealing directly with the details of the Exodus in fulfillment of the mitzvah.

Even the religiously informed will observe this mitzvah at variant levels. Some might well inject some learned discussion for a little while, while others might attempt to emulate the five sages who stayed up until dawn studying the passages of the Exodus. For this reason the individual does not make a specific blessing over the biblical mitzvah of relating the Exodus, since it is impossible for him to determine precisely the point at which he fulfills his duty. *And over an imprecise ritual, or one which we cannot observe in its entirety, or one in which any of the important attendant prescriptions is missing, we do not make a blessing!*

There is, in fact, just one precedence of a blessing prescribed over a negative situation, and that is in the Betrothal Blessing, which refers to God having "prohibited us [to cohabit with] those that are [merely] betrothed." All other blessings in our tradition are over positive activities and rituals. We must ask ourselves, therefore, whether, within the history of this festival, there is anything that could possibly explain or justify such a blessing over a negative situation and over a ritual that we cannot be sure to fulfill to the letter?

The answer is that the entire pre-history of the Exodus began with a negative element, an omission, something that was overlooked—as the *chametz*, undetected—and which, had it been located and given proper attention, would assuredly have prevented our people from having to endure centuries of slavery and oppression in an alien land, thus obviating the need for the Exodus and the entire festival of Pesach.

We refer to the way father Jacob totally overlooked the burgeoning hatred and jealousy that erupted between his youngest son, Joseph, and the rest of the brothers. When Joseph first came back with his initial tale about his brothers' conduct, Jacob should have investigated the allegations, and, if they were founded, he should have rebuked his sons and ensured that they would not repeat their evil deeds. He should have done it with tact, and without disclosing the identity of his informant. After all, the Torah makes it quite clear that "Joseph brought back an evil report *to their father*." He did not report it in his brothers' presence, so we have no reason to assume that they knew initially from whom the report had emanated. With some careful thought, Jacob could have saved the situation and maintained the peace among his sons. Unthinking, he rashly disclosed to the other brothers the identity of his informant.

This fanned the strife between them, which soon festered into harsh enmity, to the extent that both sides lost all sense of rationality. Under normal circumstances, Joseph would certainly have kept his dreams to himself.

But these were not normal circumstances. They were highly charged, and had reached a level where Joseph latched onto any circumstance that could boost his position, vindicate his righteousness, and prove the truth of his allegations by demonstrating that God had chosen him above all his older and less worthy brothers.

This, as we know, set off the chain reaction of Joseph's kidnap and sale into Egypt, leading, ultimately, to the sojourn of his brothers in that land, and the ultimate enslavement of the Israelite people. Thus, the saga of the slavery, the Exodus, and the festival of Pesach is played out against the backdrop of one man refusing to see the *chametz*, the leavening, of a potentially explosive domestic situation.

It is quite appropriate, therefore, that the very first mitzvah inaugurating this festival, which highlights, more than any other, the responsibility of parents toward their children, should symbolize our human fallibility and our frequent inability to see what is in front of our eyes. This is symbolized by the *chametz* that we cannot locate due to our frequent bias and clouded judgment in respect of our own offspring.

6

ॐ

The Symbolism of the Paschal Lamb

The keynote of the festival of Passover was the offering of the *Korban Pesach*, the Paschal lamb. Until the destruction of the second Temple it was the selection, sacrifice, and barbecue of that lamb in family groups that inaugurated the festival and, at the same time, generated the excitement and atmosphere that permeated the whole festive period. Today, only the Samaritans observe the full ritual of the *Korban Pesach*. We merely commemorate it by the roasted shank-bone on our Seder plate.

The predominant influence of the *Korban Pesach* is attested to by the significant fact that the name of that first evening's ritual—*Pesach* (Ex. 12:11)—became the more common nomenclature for the whole festival, notwithstanding the fact that the other biblical term,

Chag Ha-matzot, is a much more comprehensive term focusing upon a ritual (the eating of *matzah),* which extends over the full seven (among the Diaspora, eight) days of the festival. It might be instructive, therefore, to inquire more closely into the symbolic function of the Paschal lamb ceremonial.

An axiom of our approach is that it is inconceivable that the Israelites were commanded to go through all the paraphernalia of the taking of the lamb on tenth of Nisan, keeping it for four days, slaughtering it, and dipping hyssop branches into its blood to facilitate the daubing over the doorposts, merely in order that God might be enabled to pinpoint the Israelite homes. Did the All-seeing, omniscient God really require such an identification mark in order to help Him "pass over" their houses? A cursory reading of the way the Torah seems to be explaining the significance of the ritual (Ex. 12:12, 23) might, indeed, lead us to an affirmative answer, however philosophically and theologically perplexing.[1]

The Midrash (quoted by *Rashi* on Ex. 12:13) is equally troubled by this theological inconsistency. It attempts to resolve the problem by broadening the implication of the phrase, "And I shall see the blood and pass over you."

> *Surely everything is revealed before God! But, says the Holy One, blessed be He, I shall take cognizance of the fact that you are occupying yourselves with my commandments, and I shall pass over you.*

Thus, in a rather subtle and unconvincing shift of emphasis, the Midrash is suggesting that it was not the visual effect of the blood that was intended to serve as an instrument to enable Israel to escape divine retribution, but, rather, the more general merit of being involved in the fulfillment of one of God's directives.

This interpretation is underscored by an inference from the phrase, "And the blood shall be *for you* as a sign upon the houses" *(ibid)*. The Midrash comments: *"For you* as a sign, but not for others as a sign. From here we learn that they only smeared the blood around the inside doorposts (within the house)."[2] The Midrash is clearly attempting to reject any suggestion that the purpose of the blood was to provide *God* with information that He required regarding the Israelite occupancy of the houses.

By protesting too much, however, the Midrash is really begging the question, for, if it was the merit of merely doing *some* mitzvah *or other* that secured the safety of the occupants, then, again, we may ask why God insisted on precisely *that* particular Paschal lamb ritual, one so complex, so hedged in with regulations, and a ritual without parallel in their past religious tradition. Would not the mere offering of any sacrifice, without the attendant unique prescriptions, have constituted the *mitzvah* of obedience that the Midrash claims God required in order to justify passing over the Israelite homes? This consideration forces us to the conclusion that we cannot take this Midrash, which plays down the significance of the individual details of the Paschal lamb, as the last word on the subject. We believe that each and every one of those individual details provides us with the key to an understanding of precisely what this ritual is intended to convey. We will attempt to demonstrate that the *Korban Pesach* ritual breathes a sophisticated spirit, saturated with a rich symbolism related to the immediacy of the new national experience, identity, and consciousness that the Israelites were being called upon to affirm at that climactic moment of deliverance. We are in no way troubled by the fact that a straightforward reading of the text does seem to offer an unequivocal explanation of the purpose of the daubing of the blood, namely that God might "see the blood and pass over" Israelite homes.

It is our contention that the Torah was consciously providing a superficial explanation of the ritual that the uneducated Israelite masses could comprehend. The Torah resorts to this overtly in the context of the various other ritual components of this festival (see Ex. 12:26, 13:8, 14; Deut. 6:20). To generate a sense of awe, wonderment, understanding, and appreciation of all the details of the Passover on the part of the simple masses was regarded by the Torah as essential. Indeed, so pedagogically effective was our tradition in that direction that its efforts succeeded in providing the impetus for, and molding the style and content of, the Passover Haggadah and so much of the Seder and festival ritual.

We find difficulty with the popular interpretation of the *Korban Pesach* ritual, which views it as a supreme test of Israelite faith, to ascertain whether they could summon sufficient courage to seize that symbol of the Egyptian deity and risk any violent repercussions on the part of the Egyptians.[3]

Even a cursory reading of Exodus chapter 12 makes it quite clear that the ritual of the *Korban Pesach* is not introduced in the spirit of a test or challenge. The possible or probable reaction of the Egyptians to the taking of their lamb is nowhere alluded to, or even hinted at. It is an act of significance for Israel alone. Furthermore, if it was merely a test of Israelite defiance of their overlords, then the mere taking and sacrificing of the lamb would serve the whole of that purpose. There would be absolutely no reason for garnishing that demonstration of courage and faith with a whole set of unrelated, subsidiary regulations governing the way the meat of the sacrifice is subsequently to be eaten. Additionally, if viewed as a test, there could likewise be created a certain polarity between the overall purpose of the ritual, which would be a *national* demonstration (Israel as "the people of God" demonstrating their faith in Him and justifying thereby their "collective" liberation), and the details of the ritual that have a clearly circumscribed *domestic* complexion ("a lamb for each household").

Furthermore, whenever the Torah sets out to administer a test, whether at the individualistic or national level, it does not withhold the fact that it is a test: "And the Lord *tested* Abraham" (Gen. 22:1); "There He put them to *the test*" (Ex. 15:25); "That I might *test* him whether he will walk in my law or not" (Ex. 16:4); "Do not be afraid, God has come only *to test* you" (Ex. 20:20). The false prophet who might attempt to lead Israel astray in the future is described as a manifestation of "the Lord your God *testing* you" (Deut. 13:4). In every example the same verb, *nisah* ("to test"), is employed. It is significantly missing, however, from the context of the *Korban Pesach*. That clearly was not intended as a test.

Any such attempt to explain the *Korban Pesach* as a test—a means of obtaining sufficient merit for Israel in order to justify her redemption—breaks down in the wake of authoritative rabbinic traditions, deeply rooted in biblical evidence (Ez. 20:6–8), which suggest that the Israelites could in no way "merit" redemption, since they never abandoned their addiction to idolatry. On the verse (Deut. 4:34), "Did ever a god attempt to come and take for himself one nation from out of the midst of another nation *(goy mikkerev goy)*?" the Midrash, alluding to the fact that the Torah tars both Israel and Egypt with the same brush (calling them both *goy)*, observes, "Just as they [the Egyptians] were idolaters, so were they [Israel] idolaters."[4] Thus, the single act of taking and slaying the lamb and smearing its blood on the doorposts could hardly have been regarded as sufficiently meritorious to counteract the grievous sin of idolatry.

Nachmanides explains the emphatic repetition of the references to God "hearing Israel's cry," "remembering His Covenant," "seeing the Children of Israel," "knowing [their plight]" (Ex. 2:24–25), "knowing their pain" (3:7), and so forth, as reflective of the fact that although the predetermined time of servitude had been completed, *yet they were not worthy to be redeemed*, as explained by the prophet Ezekiel. It was solely on account of their heart-rending cries that God was moved mercifully to accept their prayers. Hence the repetition of these references.[5]

This point is made even more strongly by Rabbi Simcha Bunim Sofer of Pressburg in his commentary, *Sha'arei Simchah:* "Their deliverance was exclusively miraculous . . . It cannot be logically understood, other than that it was the desire and favour of the Holy One, blessed be He, like a statute which has no reason or rationale."[6] In other words, the redemption was not a reward; it was an act of divine grace and mercy, the fulfillment of a promise to the Patriarchs. If attributable to any cause, it is to the *zekhut avot*, the merit of the righteous progenitors of the nation.

Having rejected the notion of the *Korban Pesach* as a test, and having recognized the importance of understanding the purpose of its individual component regulations, we must now address ourselves to the problem of attempting to discover precisely what the purpose and objective of that ritual was, and how each of its individual rituals and regulations served to foster and enhance that basic purpose.

As is appropriate in the context of this inquiry into *ta'amei ha-mitzvot* (the rationale of our laws), we shall commence with the view of Maimonides, who, in his *Guide of the Perplexed,*[7] offers an explanation for the killing of the Paschal Lamb:

Scripture tells us, according to the version of Onkelos, that the Egyptians worshipped Aries, and therefore abstained from killing sheep, and held shepherds in contempt (see Gen. 46:34) . . . Thus the very act which is considered by the heathen as the greatest crime is the means of approaching God and obtaining His pardon for our sins.

This is also the reason why we were commanded to kill a lamb on Passover, and to sprinkle the blood thereof outsides on the gates.[8] We had to free ourselves of evil doctrines and to proclaim the opposite, namely that the very act which was then considered as being deserving of death would be the cause of deliverance from death. Thus they were rewarded for performing openly a service every part of which was objected to by the idolaters.

Maimonides is not suggesting here that because the Egyptians worshipped sheep and refrained from slaughtering them, that it was *for that reason* a test of the Israelites' faith and courage to see whether they were prepared to perpetrate an act of blasphemy by killing the Egyptian god. The point being made is that to take their idolatrous symbol and to sacrifice it to the true God is a manifest and worthy renunciation of idolatry, and a denial of the capability of the false god to exact vengeance for such an act. This consideration heightens the effectiveness of this particular animal as a sin offering, enabling Israel, through the implicit denial of other gods, to achieve greater proximity to God "and obtain His pardon for our sins."

Moses Nachmanides[9] offers but a slight variation of Maimonides' interpretation:

The reason for this command is that the mazal *(Zodiacal sign) of Aries is in the height of its power in the month of Nisan, since it is in the ascendancy at that time. Hence the command to slaughter the lamb and devour it, in order to demonstrate that it was not as a result of our [astrological] fortune (*mazal*) that we were enabled to leave Egypt, but by direct decree of the Most High. And according to the opinion of our [Midrashic] Sages, that the Egyptians used to worship the lamb, how much more would this command demonstrate that God had cast down their gods and neutralized the strength attributed to them, since He was unique in His pre-eminence?*[10]

One of the difficulties with these interpretations is that they force us totally to divorce the act of taking and slaughtering the lamb from the components of the ritual regulations associated with the eating of it. For that reason, Maimonides is constrained to offer a totally different, practical rationale for the latter (which we shall presently discuss), whereas the whole tenor of the biblical presentation suggests an integrated ritual symbolism. We are also uncomfortable at the thought that, in the light of the nation's acknowledged idolatrous propensity,[11] they should be granted the merit of deliverance purely on the basis of a charade, namely, *after having been instructed* to perform a sacrificial token of a monotheistic allegiance that they manifestly had not hitherto acknowledged in thought or deed.

We also find difficult Maimonides' view of the *Korban Pesach* as a type of sin offering for idolatry,[12] since the concept of an offering as an atonement for sin did not exist before the giving of the Torah.

Furthermore, Moses' initial excuse to Pharaoh for insisting that the Hebrews leave the country was that they needed to celebrate a festival to God (Ex. 10:9). For this, he alleged, they had to go into the desert, since, the implication was, they could not offer their sacrifices in an idolatrous and unclean land. How, then, can the *Korban Pesach* possibly be construed as a sacrifice, "a sin-offering," which the Israelites offered in Egypt?

Again, the *Korban Pesach* could not possibly be placed into the category of a sin-offering *(chatat)*, since the basic principle governing the latter is that it is prescribed for the *unintentional* commission of sins for which, if perpetrated intentionally, the biblical punishment imposed is "divine excommunication" *(karet)*. This principle could not be applied to the Israelite situation, since, in the first place, their idolatry could hardly be justified as unintentional, and, secondly, the actual punishment for the intentional public perpetration of idolatry is not *karet*, but death by stoning *(s'kilah)*.[13]

Even if some argument were to be adduced in order to place their idolatry into the category of the unintentional, on the grounds that the Torah had not yet been given and religious culpability was not yet accepted, the lamb of the *Korban Pesach* could still not serve as the sin-offering for this category of unintentional offense. For the Torah prescribes exclusively "a young bullock . . . with its meal offering and drink offering, and one he-goat" (Num. 15:24) as the sin-offering for idolatry committed unintentionally.[14] A lamb is unacceptable.[15]

Another problem associated with Maimonides' view of the *Korban Pesach* as a sin-offering is that for a nation steeped in idolatry to be made to go through a charade of making atonement through sacrifice *without any pre-scribed confession*, would be equivalent, in Rabbinic parlance, to "one who immerses himself in the *mikveh* (ritual bath) while holding a defiling reptile in his hand."[16]

We are therefore forced into a position where we must seek a less problematic explanation.

II.

Before proceeding to our own suggestion as to the underlying symbolism of the *Korban Pesach*, we shall direct our attention to an important problem regarding the very first of its biblical prescriptions, which hitherto has not been adequately explained, namely, why the Israelites were commanded to take the lamb on the tenth day of the month (Ex. 12:3) and to keep it in their homes for four full days (v. 6) until the eve of their departure. Secondly, why this law only applied to the first Passover, and was not carried over as part of the subsequent years' ritual.

For obvious reasons, Maimonides does not deal with this law when attempting to explain the various

LET MY PEOPLE GO

Paschal lamb prescriptions as symbolizing "haste." This particular prescription would not only be an exception to his rule, but would undermine it altogether! In point of fact, however, Maimonides was correct in omitting this from the list; for we believe that its rationale is a practical one, totally unrelated to the other prescriptions regarding its slaughter and ritual consumption.

The problem of the four-day pre-selection occupied the minds of our sages. Rabbi Matya ben Heresh provides the classical answer:

> The prophet Ezekiel said, "And I passed over you, and I saw you and behold your time was a time of love" (Ez. 16:8)—that is, the time had arrived to fulfill the promise (made out of "love") that God had made to Abraham, that He would redeem his children. They, however, possessed no mitzvot in which to engage in order to merit redemption, as it is said (ibid. v. 7): "You were naked and bare . . ." This means "naked of mitzvot." Therefore God gave them two mitzvot—the [daubing of the] blood of the Paschal lamb and the blood of circumcision[17]—so that they might merit redemption.[18] Hence it states (ibid. v. 6), "When I passed over you, I saw you wallowing in your blood (bedamayikh) [The Hebrew is couched in the plural]—indicative of two kinds of blood (that of the lamb and that of circumcision)."[19] Hence the Torah required the lamb to be taken four days before it was due to be slaughtered, since reward can only be earned by the performance of deeds.[20]

56

A. M. Silbermann, in his popular translated edition of *Rashi's* Commentary, appositely notes that Rabbi Matya's statement does not, in fact, give a direct reply to the question why they had to take the lamb four days previous.[21]

He understands the Midrash as intending to suggest that, in addition to the "two *mitzvot*," God was giving them here a third instruction—to take the lamb on the tenth of the month—in order that they might augment their merit still further by showing obedience to this request also. The only objection to this interpretation is that the sages should have enumerated this directive, in addition to the other two, and specified *three mitzvot* that God gave them in order to gain merit! Furthermore, Silbermann's suggestion still begs the question, for we are still in the dark as to why the lamb had to be taken just *four* days before. There must surely be some significance in that particular period of time!

The Midrash[22] continues by quoting an objection raised by Rabbi Eliezer Ha-Kappar. He is uneasy about the suggestion that Israel had no merit at all (hence the extra *mitzvah* of taking the lamb four days earlier, in order to augment the extent of her obedience). He draws attention to the well-known tradition that Israel's redemption was earned on account of four unique demonstrations of national identity and moral integrity:

> They were above suspicion as regards immorality and
> tale-bearing (viz. they respected confidentiality and
> possessed other fine traits of character), they clung
> tenaciously to their native Hebrew language and did not

exchange their Hebrew names for Egyptian ones (viz. they retained their cultural identity and independence).

Rabbi Eliezer Ha-Kappar cannot accept, therefore, that any further *mitzvot* were necessary in order to boost Israel's merit, and thus he is constrained to offer an alternative explanation of why they were told to take the lamb four days before. He sees its rationale in the context of Israel's sin of idolatry, which, he demonstrates by various proof texts, is as heinous as all the other sins of the Torah put together. From this consideration he proceeds to explain the import of the rather vague imperative, "withdraw *(mishkhu)* and take for yourselves a lamb" (Ex. 12:21). The meaning, according to Rabbi Eliezer, is "withdraw from idolatry *(mishkhu yedeikhem me'avodah zarah)* and cleave exclusively to God's commandments."

Thus, Eliezer Ha-Kappar's answer to the problem of the pre-selection of the lamb is that the four days were intended to give the Israelites a "cooling-off period," a chance to allow the process of rejection of idolatry to take its natural course, and a period in which to achieve a mental separation, enabling the nation to reflect upon the new monotheistic commitment that it was being called upon to embrace.

Once again, however, it will be apparent that while this explanation also succeeds in offering a reason why the *Korban Pesach* had to be taken some time before it was sacrificed, it still does not shed any light on why just *four days* before!

The explanation we now offer has the benefit of simplicity. It is our view that the midrashic tradition of the commingling of the blood of circumcision with the blood of the Paschal lamb provides us with the key to this problem. Certainly the law that no uncircumcised person may eat the *Korban Pesach* (Ex. 12:48) was, in effect, a directive for the Israelites to perform circumcision. The divine purpose was clearly that the fulfillment of both *mitzvot*, circumcision and the slaughtering of the lamb, should follow each other in the closest proximity. This may be inferred from the fact that, although God communicated the laws of the Passover on the *first* day of the month,[23] the ritual was not to commence until ten days later. Circumcision was an essential element in the regulations governing participation in this first Passover, so it may be presumed that it should also be observed in *the context of the period of ritual activity,* namely between the tenth and fourteenth of the month.

The close association, and the desirability of achieving proximity, between the performance of circumcision and the slaughtering of the Paschal lamb is also apparent from the fact that Joshua waited to circumcise the new generation, born in the desert, until just before the celebration of Passover (see Josh. 5:7–10). Now, it was generally acknowledged that three full days are required in order to recuperate after the circumcision operation.[24] The Israelites could not therefore have been expected to undertake the physically demanding process of selection (that is, finding a lamb of the requisite size for the exact number of participants) and examination (to ensure that it was without any blemish) while they were still weak from the circumcision. It follows, therefore, that, in order to have the lamb ready for roasting on the fourteenth of Nisan, immediately after their recovery from the three days of their indisposition, it would have to be selected, waiting and ready, on the day before the circumcision took place, that is on the tenth day of the month![25]

It will now be obvious why this law requiring the lamb to be selected on the tenth of Nisan only applied to the very first Passover in Egypt, and was not carried over as part of the subsequent years' regular ritual. Since it was introduced as an immediate, practical necessity, to facilitate the wholesale circumcision that was about to take place, it was obviously unnecessary in subsequent years, since the whole nation had already been circumcised, and circumcision had already taken its place as an automatic religious ritual performed on the eighth day after birth.

III.

We have already mentioned that Maimonides expounds the purpose of the detailed ritual regulations governing the *Korban Pesach* in terms of "haste":

> *The reason of the particular laws concerning the Passover lamb is clear. It was eaten roasted by fire (Ex. 12:8–9) in one house, and without breaking the bones thereof (v. 46). In the same way as the Israelites were com-*

manded to eat unleavened bread, because they could prepare it hastily, so they were commanded, for the sake of haste, *to roast the lamb, because there was not sufficient time to boil it, or to prepare other food; even the delay caused by breaking the bones to extract their marrow was prohibited. The one principle laid down for all these laws is, "You shall eat it in haste" (Ex. 12:11).*

But when haste is necessary the bones cannot be broken up, nor can parts of the animal be sent from house to house, for this would mean that the messenger would have to suffer a delay before eating his own portion on his return. This would defeat the whole purpose and would frustrate the requirement of speed and haste in order that none should be too late to leave Egypt with the main body of the people, and be thus exposed to the attacks and evil designs of the enemy . . .

Each Passover lamb was only eaten by those who had previously agreed to consume it together, in order that people should be anxious to procure it, and should not rely on friends, relations, or on chance, without themselves taking any trouble about it before Passover.

The reason of the prohibition that the uncircumcised should not eat of it (Ex. 12:48) is explained by our Sages as follows:

The Israelites neglected circumcision during their long stay in Egypt, in order to make themselves appear like the Egyptians.[26] When God gave them the commandment of the Passover, and ordered that no one could kill the Passover lamb unless he, his sons, and all the male persons in his household were circumcised . . . all performed this commandment.[27]

A close examination of this passage will reveal a number of difficulties associated with Maimonides' thesis. First and foremost, he is unable to sustain a comprehensive explanation of *all* the ritual regulations by expounding the single rationale of haste. He can sustain this explanation only as regards three of the regulations: (1.) that it must be roasted by fire; (2.) that it must be eaten in one house; and (3.) that none of its bones may be broken. He is constrained to offer a totally different rationale, however, for two of the other regulations: (1.) that the lamb could be eaten only by those who had previously arranged to participate (rationale: to stimulate personal involvement in the *mitzvah*) and (2.) that the uncircumcised were unable to participate (rationale: to resuscitate the neglected covenant of circumcision).

Secondly, he totally ignores some of the other equally important biblical regulations governing the *Korban Pesach*, making no attempt to demonstrate how they may be harmonized with his overall rationale. The significant omissions are the following:

(1) No alien may join in the ritual (Ex. 12:43). The term "alien" *(ben nekhar)* was understood by rabbinic tradition to refer particularly to a *Yisra'el mumar*, a Jewish apostate.[28]

(2) Although the celebration was to be confined in the first instance to each household *(seh labayit)*, yet the list of participants may be extended to include a neighbor if the household is too small to finish an entire lamb (Ex. 12:4).

(3) The punishment of *karet* ('severance from the community') for failure to observe the ritual of the

Korban Pesach. The fact that this feature is referred to only later, in the context of the law of *Pesach Sheni*, the Second Passover, (Num. 9:13), is no reason for overlooking its significance, especially since it is one of only two positive *mitzvot* for the willful neglect of which the punishment of *karet* is imposed.[29] The other is circumcision, and it can be no coincidence that they are both so inextricably interconnected in this ritual of the *Korban Pesach*, a point which Maimonides did not note.

(4) The fact that the Torah debars specifically one "who is unclean by reason of *contact with a dead body*" (Num. 9:10) from participating in the *Korban Pesach* ritual, even though one unclean *(tamei)* as a result of any of the other agencies of defilement[30] is similarly debarred,[31] suggests that the former has to have a particular significance in the context of the symbolism of the *Korban Pesach!*

We have now reached the stage where we must postulate a new symbolism as underlying this ritual, one that will serve to unify *all* the individual laws, wedding them all into one integrated mosaic.

We must acknowledge, however, that the symbolic meaning we are about to attribute to the *Korban Pesach* does have strong points of contact with interpretations that have already been expounded by some past scholars. Theodor H. Gaster, for example, explains the essence of the Paschal lamb ritual as a *communal meal*, part of "a common pattern of seasonal festivals in many parts of the world." Its basic purpose, says Gaster, "is to re-cement the bonds of kindred and community at the beginning of a new agricultural cycle."[32]

While we will also explain the eating of the *Korban Pesach* as a communal meal, our specific contribution lies in the particular emphasis we detect as underlying this meal, and particularly in our demonstration of the way each of the individual biblical prescriptions reflects and enhances that basic symbolic message.

IV.

The link between circumcision and the *Korban Pesach* ritual—a link echoed by rabbinic exegesis of Ezekiel 16:6—suggests at the outset that they share a similar symbolic objective, namely to serve as outward signs of a covenanted relationship shared by all their initiates. Just as circumcision is a rite of passage into the community and its fellowship, so is the *Korban Pesach* a symbol of, and an attempt to heighten, the sense of unity and shared kinship experienced by all participants in the ritual.

This central message, underlying the communal meal of the Paschal lamb, was particularly timely at that moment when the Israelites prepared to leave Egypt and, for the first time in their history, take their destiny into their own hands as an independent nation in search of their historic roots in the land promised to their founding fathers.

It is worthy of note that the instructions regarding the lamb are introduced by the phrase *dabru 'el kol 'adat yisra'el* ("Speak to all *the congregation* of Israel"). The noun *'edah* ("congregation") is introduced here for the first rime as a designation of the Israelites. It is derived from the root *ya 'ad*, "to assemble together by appointment," "to act concertedly."[33] The inference is, clearly, that the ritual that they are about to perform, one for which they "assemble by appointment" and "act in concert," is calculated to invest the hitherto disparate "fathers' houses" and tribes with the status, unity, and identity of "a congregation."

That their national and fraternal bonds should have needed to be strengthened just at this time is not at all surprising, for they were about to embark upon a new national experience calculated to put the greatest strain upon their sense of unity and community. This new challenge would come in the wake of liberation.

There is a keener challenge contained in freedom than in slavery. The slave is disciplined and controlled from without. He is restricted; but the absence of choice does have its positive dimension in that he is protected from the dilemmas and decisions that free men must make regarding the direction of their own lives and destinies.

An enslaved nation is a fairly cohesive entity, bound together by strong psychological and emotional cords, united in a common bond of suffering and a common dream of deliverance, unified by their hostility towards the common oppressor and linked by an empathy for their fellow sufferers. In such a situation the sense of kinship and brotherhood is self-generating. The roots go deeper and deeper, nourished by the trauma of the common experience.

Freedom, on the other hand, is, ironically, the greatest threat to all this cohesion and unity. Freedom generates diversity of ideas, patterns of behavior, social stratification, and religious consciousness. Freedom dilutes the unique *esprit de corps* generated by the oppressive experience. Freedom dissipates insularity and dissolves clannishness and chauvinism. Freedom disarms, disperses, and diversifies.

This was the threat that suddenly loomed large upon the widening horizon of the Israelites as they contemplated the Exodus. This was the great and inevitable danger, alone capable of thwarting the divine aim of molding the Hebrews into a nation, a unified entity.

To try and forestall this threat, God made Israel enter into a symbolic "covenant of unity," immediately prior to the Exodus, to be reaffirmed annually (though with some minor modifications to suit the change of circumstances).[34] This was the ritual of the *Korban Pesach*, a ritual whose aim was to foster and intensify cohesiveness, fraternal association, and community spirit.

A communal meal was regarded in antiquity as the most effective way of cementing unity and promoting fellowship. For that reason it figured prominently in the ritual of the Essene community, as reflected in the Dead Sea Scrolls, as well as among the select *chavurah* (fellowship) circles of the Pharisaic community.[35] Its origin may well have been inspired by the fellowship groups

formed to enjoy the Paschal lamb, a view first enunciated by A. Geiger.[36] Indeed, the Paschal lamb fellowship groups are known in rabbinic literature precisely
by that very term, *chavurah* (fellowship).

The origin of the rabbinic institution of *Eiruvei
Chatzerot*—the symbolic joining together of all the
houses that share a common courtyard into one notional domain, in order to facilitate carrying on the
Sabbath from one house to another via the courtyard—
was also attributed by Geiger to those *chavurah* fraternity circles. The *Eruv* is established by all householders
depositing some food at the home of one of their
members, creating thereby a common dining room (an
extension of their individual homes), and enabling
them to carry in a (notional) common domain. The
communal meal was an important element in *chavurah*
circles, symbolizing their special relationship as initiated brothers of a common fraternity.

A number of Pharisaic groups of the Second Commonwealth shared this emphasis on the meal as a
means of expressing their fellowship and unity of
purpose. Because of its special significance, as a symbol
of fraternity, one group in particular—the "pure-minded
of Jerusalem" (*nekiyei hada'at biyrushalayim*)—would
not sit at table with strangers.[37] Interestingly, the English word *companion* means, literally, "those who eat
bread [Latin: *panis*] together."

That the slaughtering and partaking of the *Korban
Pesach* was intended to emphasize the spirit of "community" is also indicated by the overemphatic designation of *kehal 'adat yisra'el* ("the assembling of the

congregation of Israel") in Exodus 12:6. So unusual was this threefold designation that early rabbinic tradition took it for granted that some special teaching underlay its usage. They consequently employed it as a textual basis for a special procedure whereby the slaughtering of the Paschal lambs, and the accompanying ritual in the Temple precincts, had to be divided into three separate ceremonies, even if the numbers did not warrant this. Each ceremony corresponded to *kehal*, *'adat*, and *yisra 'el*, respectively.[38]

That practical rabbinic application apart, from a textual point of view this emphasis serves clearly to underline the basic intention of this whole ritual. It was to create "an assembly" and "a congregation" out of an "Israel" that had hitherto been merely a disparate group of individuals united by the rather loose cords of a common ancestry. The intention was that, from this moment and forever more, their sense of unity and fellowship should be generated not by historical, but by existential, considerations. The active participation of each individual member of the new community—men, women, children, and circumcised slaves and strangers (Ex. 12:48)—in the ritual of the *Korban Pesach*, was the clearest demonstration of this existential significance of every individual as an active, responsible, authentic, and valued brother-member of the Israelite community, in his or her own right, and not merely as a featureless cog in "the anonymity of the social collective."[39] Any fears at that moment, when the tribal and family units were about to merge into that of a broader based and less parochial *national* entity, that the individual might lose his identity and sense of worth were to be dispelled by this ritual.

Support for this concept of the *Korban Pesach* as a symbol of fellowship is also forthcoming from our early rabbinic sources, where this ritual becomes the very *locus classicus* for the idea of Israel as one fraternal unit. Each member is responsible for the next and therefore able to represent his fellow's religious interests and act, accordingly, as his spiritual representative. Thus, on the above phrase "And all the assembly of the congregation of Israel shall slaughter it," the Talmud appositely asks, "Does the whole community actually slaughter?" Surely this task is left to the slaughterers! But from here we may infer the principle that "a man's agent is as himself."[40] This legal principle, with ramifications in so many areas of halakhah, is predicated upon this central concept of the nation as one fraternal unit.

This concept also finds expression in a significant gloss that *Targum Yonatan* adds to his rendering of the verse, "And if the household be too small to manage a whole lamb" (Ex. 12:4). Yonatan adds, "If there is less than a *minyan of ten,* sufficient to manage a whole lamb." This prerequisite of a *minyan* to celebrate the *Korban Pesach* ritual finds an echo in the Talmud, which observes that "there was never a Paschal lamb eaten by less than ten people."[41] The number ten is clearly not arbitrary, but represents in our tradition the basic microcosm of the community, the *minyan*. Thus, in this regulation we have a reinforcement of our basic concept of the *Korban Pesach* as a symbol of the unity of the entire Israelite fraternity.

Another explanation of the necessity for such a ritual demonstration of fraternity just before their flight from Egypt takes account of the "mixed multitude" (*eirev rav*) who were agitating to take advantage of the opportunity for escape that the Israelites now offered (Ex. 12:38; Num. 11:4). Harry Orlinsky tells us that:

> *tens of thousands of workers, natives of many countries and members of different ethnic groups, labored for the Egyptian state. Already in the fifteenth century, as a result of the military conquests of Amenhotep II in Syria and Palestine, large numbers of Semitic and non-Semitic captives of war . . . were brought to Egypt as state slaves . . . many of whom were eager to escape from slavery.*[42]

Since the Exodus was intended exclusively as the fulfillment of the Israelites' destiny, as promised to the Patriarchs (Ex. 6:3–4), and since the commitment to God and His law, as well as the covenanted relationship, was to embrace them alone, and not their fellow travelers of the "mixed multitude," it was obviously necessary, therefore, to hold a ceremony of initiation, in the form of circumcision followed by *Korban Pesach* fellowship ritual, to help close ranks and confer status upon the true sons of Abraham, in order to exclude the rest. An initiation ceremony is as much to identify and exclude the outsider as it is to designate the members of the fraternity.

We are now ready to analyze the components of the *Korban Pesach* ritual in order to see how they help, individually and collectively, to promote the central motivation of the fraternity and unity of Israel.

The antithesis of fraternity is individualism; hence our ritual eschews any such expression. For this reason no Israelite was permitted to eat alone, even if he was capable of consuming an entire lamb by himself.[43] It had to be eaten in a *chavurah,* a social context, a microcosm of the nation as a cohesive unit.

Since the purpose of the ritual was to intensify the sense of the cohesiveness of the whole community, it follows that *all* members of the community, even if their religious or social status was of a lesser degree—such as women,[44] children old enough to eat of its meat,[45] and circumcised slaves—were obliged to participate in the *Korban Pesach* ritual.

Where members of one household could not manage to consume a whole lamb, they were to join with neighbors. The term used to describe the latter is problematic, in that it seems to be tautological: "a neighbor, who is near to his house" *(shekheino ha-karov 'el beito).* The *Mekhilta* attempts to explain away the problem by suggesting that the additional clarification— "who is near to his house"—comes to include the permissibility of sharing the ritual with a family that lives above, on the roof (a first-floor apartment?). This clarification would be necessary since *shekheino* generally suggests a next-door neighbor. It need hardly be pointed out, however, that the biblical tent-dwellers to whom the Torah here addressed itself (even though the ritual was to be preserved down the ages) would hardly have known of first-floor neighbors!

Seforno, obviously unhappy with the above explanation, suggests another justification for the phrase "who is near to his house." He points out that there were Egyptians living as next-door neighbors to many Israelite homes. In that situation, the Torah points out that the Israelite nearest to his home (ha-karov 'el beito) is to be considered as his shekheino ("next-door neighbor").

We consider, however, that the tautology is more apparent than real, for the Torah may here be seen to be actually recommending the type of neighbor with whom one might—or might not—join for this celebration. It had to be "a neighbor who is close to one's home," namely a family with whom one also shared a close bond of fraternal friendship.

This extra, emotional nuance of the term shakhein is emphasized in the halakhic context of a dinah debar metzar, the primary right of a neighbor to have first refusal of a field that is being offered for sale.[46] The definition of "neighbor" is obviously of great practical significance here. M. Isserles comments: "Some say that a shakhein is only a neighbor with whom one has a friendly relationship. Simply living next door to a person means nothing (it does not justify the designation shakhein)." The Tur believes that an even deeper relationship is suggested by the term, namely (1.) a friend (2.) with whom one engages in regular dealings and transactions.[47]

We see, therefore, how the Torah wishes here to promote the idea of unity and fraternity by insisting that those gathered as chavurah, to enjoy the Korban

Pesach, should themselves be bound in an emotional bond of unity, strong enough to symbolize the ideal to which the nation as a whole from then on had to aspire.

We can now understand why the eating of the lamb was restricted, in the first instance, to each individual household. A family home is the most compact symbol of unity and fraternity. Only where the lamb could not be totally consumed was it permitted to extend the unit of participation to include *shekheino ha-karov 'el beito*—those who qualified to be regarded as "extended family."

We view the prescription that those participating had to be invited in advance, and the size of lamb determined by their number, as serving this central purpose of promoting harmony, peace, and unity. There would then be no squabbling over the size of portion each was to receive, or worse, whether someone was or was not invited at all, for all had been pre-arranged. Harmony, unity, and cordiality were assured, and each participant was an honored guest.

This also explains why it was prohibited to move from one *chavurah* to another, an act which might certainly be construed as divisive.

The preparation of the *Korban Pesach* had also to symbolize unity. Hence it was roasted on fire, so that it would remain whole, and would not require dismembering in order to remove the blood from its various limbs.[48]

For the same reason, care had to be exercised not to break any of its bones. The breaking of bones impairs the wholeness of the entity. It symbolizes friction, division, separation: the antithesis of the spirit being promoted by this ritual.[49]

This is the probable explanation of why any meat left over from the *Korban Pesach* until the next day had to be burned in fire (Ex. 2:10). Any eating of ritual meat on the following day could be misconstrued as a separatist act. *All* had to eat the *whole* lamb at *one* time. This "concentration of time and place" is an essential feature of the symbolic message of unity and unanimity being promoted by the ritual. This was to be even further heightened by the prescription to eat the lamb "in haste" (Ex. 12:11), providing a greater concentration of activity within the shortest possible period of *time*.

It was also to be eaten fully dressed and ready for the journey: "loins girded, shoes on feet and staff in hand" (ibid). This would also ensure concentration of *place*, so that none would slip away from the ritual celebration, or even absent themselves altogether, in order to get ready for the impending Exodus. That would certainly have impaired the effect of this unique demonstration of unity. All had to be completely ready, with absolutely nothing more to do than to participate in, and be witness to, this climactic event.

This central concept may also explain why the Torah exemplified the exclusion of one who was unclean—*lanefesh*—*to a dead person*. It may be presumed that such a situation usually occurs in the case of one burying a near relative. The bereaved person could not possibly be expected to share in this ritual promotion of the idea of a unified community, since his predominant emotion would be the very opposite: He or she would be overwhelmed by a sense of loss, a void, and a feeling of depletion of his family circle. This feeling, that the unity and wholeness of the community has been impaired, is equally shared by others coming into contact with the dead, even if not directly related to them.

It goes without saying, therefore, that the *ben nekhar*—the Jewish apostate, whose actions had "estranged him from his father in heaven"—the one who had broken the ranks and impaired the *unity* of the faithful, must be excluded from participation in a ritual that sets out to promote the very ideal that he was callously undermining.

We may now appreciate why circumcision and *Korban Pesach* are the only two positive commands, the punishment for willful neglect of which is *karet*, "excision from the community." These two rituals both symbolize the unity and exclusiveness of our people, and for that reason are inextricably interwoven, as we have demonstrated. It is logical, therefore, that the punishment should fit the crime. Thus, anyone who, by disregard of these two rituals, demonstrates an unwillingness to be included within the ranks of the community, has his wish granted, and is accordingly punished by *karet*, total exclusion from it.

V.

At the outset of this chapter we emphasized the problem of interpreting the daubing of the blood on the doorposts as a signal to God to help Him distinguish the Israelite homes. Our final task, therefore, is to demonstrate how the blood of the lamb ties in with the idea of unity and fraternity, which we viewed as the central symbolic message of the entire *Korban Pesach* ritual.

Blood has always constituted a significant factor in the establishment of a covenant and in cementing a sense of kinship between people: "Blood is thicker than water." 'Among most primitives, the consanguinal kin group is characterized by a strong sense of collective solidarity, which functions to protect its individual members against assault and injury by outsiders.'[50]

It was common practice for people unrelated to each other, but wishing to establish a solemn fraternal bond between them, to enter into a blood covenant. Each member would draw blood, and the act of commingling it would make them into "blood brothers." Symbolically they henceforth shared a bond of consanguinity. Hence the Torah twice refers to *dam berit*,"the blood of the covenant" (Ex. 24:8; Zech. 9:11).

It is to the description of the blood covenant in Exodus 24:1–11 that we will turn in order to provide the key to the relationship between the eating of the *Korban Pesach* and the daubing of the blood. This describes a covenant between God and Israel, ratified by God allowing the leadership of the community an unprecedented, and never to be repeated, glimpse of His presence:

> *And they beheld the God of Israel, and beneath His feet there was the like of a paved work of sapphire stone,*

and the like of the very heaven for clearness. And upon the nobles of the children of Israel He laid not His hand, though they beheld God, and did eat and drink. (vv. 10–11)

The purpose of this covenant was to establish an eternal and indissoluble bond between God and Israel. To make it abundantly clear that no tribes, or segment of the nation, stood outside of this covenant, Moses "built an altar at the foot of the Mountain [Sinai], and erected twelve pillars, according to the twelve tribes of Israel" (v. 4). They then offered sacrifices to God, and used the blood of the sacrifices as the means of reinforcing the covenant (v. 5). "And Moses took half of the blood and put it in basins; and half of the blood he sprinkled upon the altar" (v. 6). . . . "And Moses took the blood and poured it over the people, and said: This is the blood of the covenant which the Lord has made with you" (v. 8).

S.D. Luzatto makes the following telling observation:

All of that blood should really have been poured upon the altar, for it [the sacrifice] was a gift to God. But God commanded that half of it be poured upon the people, as a gift token of loving reciprocity for the fact that they had received His Torah. It was as if they were eating from the table of the Most High. This [symbolic blood sharing] represented the meal accompanying the Covenant which God was making with them to become their God and they to become His people, to the extent that they would perform all these commands which He had just given them. For it was the custom at the inauguration of all covenants of love that the signatories ate a meal together.[51]

If we transfer all this symbolism to the *Korban Pesach* situation, we find that it represents a parallel type of covenant. A bond is being established between all members of the congregation of Israel. The *Korban Pesach* meal unites them as a people; its daubed blood makes it into a solemn and binding "blood covenant." Just as at that later covenant, after the giving of the Torah, the two main components were the presentation of blood and the symbolic meal, so did the daubing of the blood and the eating of the *Korban Pesach* reinforce that central concept of unity, kinship, loyalty, and fraternity.

There was one major difference, however, between those two covenants. The *Korban Pesach* covenant was sealed in Egypt, a land of idolatry. For this reason no altars could be constructed, upon which to sprinkle the blood. Whereas the later "blood covenant" was made in the desert, with no such impediment to the full celebration of a sacrificial ritual. Because of the absence of an altar at the *Korban Pesach* ritual, some other place had to be designated for the ritual sprinkling of the (covenant) blood.[52] The doorposts and lintels of the houses were therefore chosen. Just as the eating of the lamb was performed within each house, to symbolize absolute unity, so the blood was sprinkled around its entrance to reinforce that same message. The blood outside mirrored the blood relationship within the house, extending the bond of consanguinity to encompass the whole national entity. Like circumcision, it was a physical manifestation of an emotional bond.

The Midrash[53] deprecates the fact that during the whole of the forty years of wandering in the desert the Israelites only observed one other Paschal lamb celebration, on the first anniversary of the Exodus (Num. 9:1–5). This might well have been the divine intention, and may be read into the wording of the command: "When the Lord brings you into the land of the Canaanites . . . you shall keep this service" (Ex. 13:5). The single attempt to repeat the Korban Pesach ritual in the desert, a year later, may well have proved most uninspiring, and for that reason was not repeated. How, indeed, could they have attempted so soon to recreate the atmosphere and tension of that unique event, which was still so vivid in their memories? It could not have felt other than a hollow charade. Furthermore, in the light of our understanding of the purpose of this ritual, an annual reaffirmation of the nation's sense of unity would hardly have been necessary while they all lived together, in the closest of proximity, taking up fixed encampment positions in the desert. After all, their unity and fraternal bonds were not threatened until the tribes arrived in the Promised Land and pursued their own independent aspirations. Only then was the message of the Korban Pesach really required.

Just as the sharing of an entire roasted animal betokened the absolute unity of the chavurah participants, and just as the latter represented the microcosm of the nation, so any animal that is purposely cut in pieces would symbolize the very opposite state: division, separation, and disunity.

In this way we may explain the symbolism of the "covenant between the pieces" (Gen. 15). The divided parts (vv. 9–10) symbolized Abraham's scattered seed: "strangers in a land that is not theirs." The pieces were placed opposite each other, symbolizing separate identity and lack of national cohesion. The Israelites would live, each one opposite his fellow, but they would not constitute a single entity. The divine promise was, however, that after the four hundred years had elapsed, they would become a nation, unified in their service of God. Hence the divine fire ("for the Lord thy God is a devouring fire" [Deut. 4:24]), passing between the pieces, acts as the unifying force, absorbing and uniting all the disparate components. Abraham's pieces, consumed by fire, and the *Korban Pesach*, roasted in fire, represent, respectively, the symbolic promise and its fulfillment.

According to our exposition of this ritual, all its individual laws and prescriptions will be seen to form a perfectly integrated symbolic mosaic, providing and reinforcing, over and over again, the single message of unity. Even the moment chosen by God to set the Exodus in motion promoted this idea: "And it came to pass *at* midnight" (Ex. 12:29). God established a perfect equality and equilibrium between both halves of that night of destiny. The cosmic forces enjoyed the same harmony as that which characterized the unity of God and Israel, and of Israelite and fellow Israelite.

NOTES

1. An interesting historical explanation as to the reason why the lamb had to be taken on the tenth of Nisan, which at the same time provides a rationale for its having to be kept for four days in the Israelite homes, is offered by the Midrash *Lekach Tov* (on Ex. 12:6):

> God wished to hint to them thereby that the Israelites would, in the future, cross the Jordan on that same day. Hence it states, "And the people came forth from the Jordan on the tenth day of the first month" (Josh. 4:19). Let the reward for having taken the Paschal lamb be added to that for taking the stones from the Jordan.

Thus the combined merit, with which the tenth of Nisan was mystically invested, made it, in rabbinic eyes, a day that was propitious for securing deliverance.

2. See *Rashi ad loc.*

3. The notion that the taking of the lamb was to demonstrate that they had no fear of their Egyptian masters was suggested by *Targum Yonatan*: "It shall be tied up and guarded by you until the fourteenth day of this month" (Ex. 12:6)— *that you may demonstrate that you are not afraid of what the Egyptians might do when they see it.*

4. Mid. Mekhilta, *Pischa (Bo)*, 5.

5. Nachmanides, Commentary on Ex. 2:25.

6. *Sha'arei Simchah* (Sinai ed.) 1959, p. 229 (on Ex. 12:24).

7. Maimonides, *Guide*, III, ch. 46 (Friedlander ed. p. 227).

8. Maimonides seems to be rejecting here the midrashic view (see Note 2) that the blood was sprinkled only indoors.

Maimonides may well have regarded the Midrash as merely polemical, calculated to preempt any charge that the Israelite God actually required human help in order to locate the Israelite homes. Significantly, *Targum Yonatan* injects a gloss into its rendering of Ex. 12:7 to the effect that the blood was placed "on the outside" *(mil'bar)*. This must have been the earlier, and original, tradition, changed subsequently for the polemical reason we have suggested.

9. Nachmanides, commentary on Ex. 12:3.

10. Since in the very month of his ascendancy, the god Aries would be shown to have been impotent, unable to prevent the Israelites treating the lamb with disdain. See *Chizkuni ad loc.*

11. See Note 4.

12. See especially his statement, "Thus, the very act which is considered by the heathen as the greatest crime, is the means of approaching God and *obtaining His pardon for our sins.* This is also the reason why we were commanded to kill a lamb on Passover" *(Guide,* p. 227).

13. The punishment of *karet* is imposed only on an *individual* who intentionally serves idols. Where it is done publicly, before two witnesses, the punishment is stoning *(sekilah)*. The idolatry of the Israelite nation in Egypt must certainly be placed in the latter category.

14. See Tal. *Horayot* 8a.

15. See Maimonides, *Yad, Hilkhot Ma'asei Ha-korbanot,* 1:15. It would be inconsistent for God to have required a lamb on this single occasion, to act as a sin offering, when He was about to prescribe a totally different animal for that category of sacrifice in the Torah that He was about to reveal.

16. Tal. *Ta'anit* 16a.

17. Since only one who was circumcised could participate in the *Korban Pesach* ritual (see Ex. 12:48), the Israelites, who had hitherto neglected this *mitzvah*, had to rectify it immediately and perform wholesale circumcision.

18. See *Rashi* on Ex. 12:6.

19. This midrashic interpretation is based upon the employment of a plural form, *bedamayikh* (from the noun *damim*), instead of the usual singular word for blood, *dam*. The plural suggests two types of blood: that of circumcision and that of the lamb. The Midrash *Pirkei D'Rabbi Eliezer* (ch. 29) infers this idea of two kinds of blood covenant from the repetition of the phrase, "And I said to you: Live by *your blood*; and I said to you: Live by *your blood*" (Ez. 16:6).

20. See Note 3.

21. A.M. Silbermann, *Pentateuch with Rashi's Commentary* (London, 1946), p. 236 (Appendix, note to p. 53b).

22. See Note 4.

23. See Ex. 12:2, and *Rashi ad loc.*

24. Tal. *Bava Metzi'ah 86b; Rashi* on Gen. 18:1. On Gen. 34:25 ("And it came to pass on the third day, when they were in pain") there is a dispute between *Rashi* (see his comment on Tal. *Shabb.* 86a), who is of the opinion that for the duration of the whole of the first three days following circumcision the infant is in danger, and Maimonides (*Hilkhot Shab.* 2:14) who opines that only on the third day is there a danger (of sufficient urgency to set aside Sabbath laws in order to heat water to bathe the wound). All authorities agree, however, that once the first three days have safely passed, there is no further cause for concern, and normal activity may be safely

resumed. See also Josh. 5:8 for the necessity for a recuperative period after circumcision.

25. According to the Talmud (*Pes.* 96a), even in subsequent years the lamb required to be selected on the tenth of Nisan. The practical reason that we have suggested—to recuperate from the effects of circumcision—would obviously not have been operative during subsequent years! It may be assumed, however, that that first year established a ritual precedence that, for consistency of practice (*mishum lo' plug*), was retained.

26. Maimonides' explanation here, of why the Israelites neglected circumcision, is not found in rabbinic literature, and seems to be his own conjecture, echoing the circumstances of Graeco-Roman times. The book of Maccabees (1:14) tells us that Jewish youth would "make for themselves a foreskin" in order to be eligible to run (naked) at the gymnasia. The surgical procedure of disguising the foreskin—*epispasis*—is well documented and severely denounced in rabbinic literature. Maimonides has thus superimposed a much later practice upon the conditions of ancient Egypt.

27. Maimonides, *Guide*, pp. 231–2.

28. This inference is derived from the basic meaning of *nekhar*, "to be strange," "estranged." Hence the rabbinic etymology, *shenitnakru ma'asav*: "one whose actions have estranged him from his father in heaven." This interpretation also helps to explain why the Torah specified separately both the alien and the uncircumcised (see Tal. *Yevamot* 71a).

29. See Mishnah *Keritot* 1:1; *Ibn Ezra* on Ex. 12:47.

30. Others debarred include lepers and those afflicted with gonorrhea (*zabin*). See *Pes.* 93a.

31. Tal. *Pesachim* 67a.

32. See Theodor H. Gaster, *Festivals of the Jewish Year* (N. Y., 1952), p. 33.

33. See Brown, Driver, Briggs, *A Hebrew and English Lexicon of the Old Testament*, p. 417. On the precise political connotation of the biblical term *'edah* and its significance for covenant theology, see Daniel J. Elazar, "Some Preliminary Observations On The Jewish Political Tradition," *Tradition*, 18, 3 (Fall 1980), pp. 259–63.

34. Thus, in subsequent years no daubing of the blood or eating in haste was required. These were symbols directly related to the Exodus experience; see Section V of this chapter.

35. See Millar Burrows, *The Dead Sea Scrolls* (London, 1956), p. 283 ff.

36. Tal. *Sanhedrin* 23a.

37. A. Geiger, *Juedische Zeitschrift*, ii (1863), 25; but see also C. Rabin, *Qumran Studies* (1975), 33–6.

38. See *Rashi* on Ex. 12:6; Mishnah *Pesachim* 5:5.

39. Nathan A. Scott, Jr., *Mirrors of Man in Existentialism* (Collins, 1978), p. 58.

40. Tal. *Kiddushin* 4b.

41. Tal. *Pesachim* 64b.

42. Harry M. Orlinsky, *Ancient Israel* (Cornell Univ. Press, N.Y., 1960), p. 30.

43. Maimonides, *Hilkhot Korban Pesach* 2:2; but see *Keseph Mishneh ad loc.*

44. Women are normally absolved from a positive biblical law that is confined to a specific time. *Torah Temimah* (on Ex. 12:4) suggests that the inclusion of women in this *mitzvah*

is, quite simply, because "they also were included in that miracle," when God passed over their homes and saved them also.

45. Tal. *Sukkah* 42b.

46. Shulchan Arukh, *Choshen Mishpat*, sec. 175:5.

47. *Ibid.* See comment of *Me 'irat 'Einayim.*

48. R. Jacob Culi, in his *Yalkut Me 'am Lo 'ez,* suggests that the prescription that the lambs be roasted was so that the smell of thousands of lambs burning would waft across Egypt, irritating and angering the Egyptians, and enabling the Israelites to display thereby even greater courage.

49. R. Aaron Halevi of Barcelona, in his *Sefer Ha-Chinukh,* suggests a novel reason for the prohibition against breaking bones of the *Korban Pesach:* It was in order to demonstrate the refinement and table manners expected of aristocrats in order to cultivate such qualities from the outset. See Shavel, ed. *(Mosad HaRav Kuk)* 1961, p. 73. Maimonides' explanation of why they should have wished to break the bones, namely to scrape out the marrow, is derived from *Targum Yonatan's* gloss on Ex. 12:46, 'You shall not break any bones'—in order to extract what is inside it *(bedil l'meikhul mah d'begaveh).*

50. *Encycl. Brit.* (1970 ed.), III, 803.

51. S.D. Luzzato, *Peirush Shadal* (Tel Aviv, 1966) on Ex. 24:8.

52. This explains why the daubing of the blood on the doorposts was restricted to the Passover in Egypt. In subsequent years the sanctuary and Temple altars became the places exclusively designated to receive ritual blood.

53. Mid. *Sifre, Beha'alotkha,* ch. 67.

CHAPTER
7

ᴔ

Why Moses Is Not Mentioned
in the Haggadah

Ve'avarti al eretz mitzrayim—Ani v'lo mal'ach, "And
I passed over the land of Egypt"—*I*, and not an
angel . . . *I*, and not a Seraph . . . *I*, and not a
heavenly intermediary. *I* am the One, and there is
no other." (Passover Haggadah)

The Haggadah emphasizes here the most basic principle of Judaism: that it was God, not Moses, who
brought our people out of Egypt. And it is in order to
remind us of that fact that the name of Moses is all but
suppressed (it occurs only indirectly in the context of a
single quotation) throughout the lengthy description of
the slavery and the Exodus recorded in the Haggadah.
But why should it have been deemed necessary for the
rabbis to over-emphasize in this way the exclusive role

of God, and to have to play down the role of Moses as deliverer?

Midrashic scholars have pointed out that, whenever the ancient rabbis resort to exaggerated emphasis of this kind, and seem to be manifestly protesting too much, then, more often than not, we may be sure that they had been thrown on the defensive, feeling constrained to couch their teaching in that way in order to emphasize, as strongly as they could, their antipathy to a sectarian view that deeply offended their theological sensibilities.

This particular over-emphasis bears all the hallmarks of a broadside against the new religion of Christianity that alarmed the rabbis of the early centuries greatly, not only because it was gaining converts from among assimilated Jews, but also because its basic tenet—that God could become transmuted into a human savior—was anathema to Judaism's finely honed concept of the absolute Unity of God.

It was for this reason that the sages utilized the night of Pesach, which for the Christians was already taking on a new significance as a commemoration of the Passion, or death, of their Lord, to bring forcefully home the message that there *are* no human saviors; there *are* no human intermediaries, other than God, *bichvodo uv'atzmo,* "in His glory and His unique selfhood." And it is because the rabbis felt so constrained to inveigh against the new religion that they suppressed the name and the role of Moses from the Seder story, to disabuse their co-religionists of any such notion as a human savior or intermediary.

Viewed from this anti-Christian polemical perspective, it is conceivable that another reason for the suppression of Moses' name was on account of it being so readily identifiable with the baptismal context.

We recall that it was the daughter of Pharaoh who found Moses in his crib among the bulrushes of the River Nile, where he had been hidden by his parents in the hope that he might escape the fate of all newly born Israelite boys whom the king had condemned to death by drowning. When the royal princess lifted out the babe, and decided to take him as her own, she called him *Mosheh*, which is probably the Egyptian word *msh*, meaning, simply, "little boy." The Torah, however, attributes to the name a Hebrew etymology, and explains that she called him so "because I have 'drawn him up' (*meshitihu*) out of the water" (Ex. 2:10).

In the cause of its campaign to attract converts, the Church undertook a bitter anti-Jewish polemic and made desperate attempts to convince Jews that they had been rejected by God and that Christianity was the new Israel. Its chief claim was that a New Testament and new dispensation had now superseded the "old," and that, *if properly understood and interpreted*, the Old Testament, in many passages, could be seen to foreshadow and affirm the theology of Christianity. Thus, the New Testament not only views the importance of Moses primarily in terms of his position as the precursor of Jesus, but also views his role in bringing the Israelites through the Red Sea as nothing more than a symbolic baptism:

You should understand, my brothers, that our ancestors were all under the pillar of cloud, and all of them passed through the Red Sea; and so they received baptism into the fellowship of Moses in cloud and sea . . . All these things that happened to them were symbolic. (I Corinthians 10:1ff.)

In the face of such manipulative theological expositions, it is easy to see how worried the early rabbis might well have been that, like his person, the significance of the name *Mosheh*, as one 'drawn out of the water,' might be misappropriated to yield the meaning of "the baptized one;" and it is conceivable, therefore, that the authors of the Haggadah, contemporaries of, and highly sensitive to, Christian evangelism, suppressed the name of Moses from their compilation for this most sensitive of evenings in order to frustrate the employment of any such preposterous Christological exegesis.

We hear so frequently the term "Judeo-Christian tradition," as if our two faiths were somehow an amalgam of one common and central theological axiom. But it is a mistake to imagine that there is, indeed, any such theological kinship. After all, on the very basic issue of the nature of God, we are diametrically and implacably opposed. The notion of the Trinity is a heresy, and the replacement of our Torah by a Testament that not only removes entirely the concept of *mitzvot*, but makes a human being the focus of a people's faith, is enough to dispose of any notion of a

shared heritage or tradition. To borrow Judaism's ethics, morals, festivals, and rituals, and, after reinterpret-
ing their significance, to superimpose them upon an
alien theological principle, does not create a common
religious tradition.

We are not suggesting that we should not cooper-
ate and build bridges with other faiths. We definitely
should. But we must do so in the clear knowledge that
we have totally different perspectives, and from a clear
understanding of the nature of those differences.

Ironically, just in an age when Western society is
gradually learning to tolerate multiple races, cultures,
and faiths, and to live cheek-by-jowl with them and
interact with them, with the consequence that most
Jews no longer feel the need to camouflage their beliefs
and practices—just in this age of religious tolerance
and opportunity, we have the highest recorded rate of
assimilation and intermarriage.

The message of the Haggadah's insistence that we
affirm the God we believe in has never been more
timely than in our unsettled modern age, which has
spawned a host of cults and pseudo-religions. So many
are vainly searching for the ultimate truth, putting their
faith in false prophets, gurus, and cult leaders who
preach immoral lifestyles and dangerous, life-denying
practices. So many are personality orientated, rather
than heaven directed. So many are missionary based,
and, like the "Jews for Jesus," committed to the erro-
neous belief that our two religions can be easily and
harmoniously fused without doing any injustice to either
the theology or the sensitivities of their adherents.

If our children were given a sound Jewish education, they would not seek spirituality and salvation in alternative cults. And Pesach is, truly, the festival of Jewish education, when we focus on the questions children ask, and on the importance of giving them appropriate and informed answers. Pesach is the time to review whether or not we are rooting our children's emotions in the solid bedrock of a full Jewish experience and a vibrant home life. It is the time for our communities to organize exciting and informative programs for all levels, so that they can truly say to the younger generation, *Kol dikhfin yeisei veyeichol*, "Let all who are hungry come and partake."

8

The Four Cups of Wine

There is much scholarly discussion as to the origin of wine as a sacred draught and its role in the sanctification of religious rituals. Clearly Christianity borrowed its use from Judaism, and invested it with a theological significance as representing the blood of their savior. With that association in the forefront of their minds, the blood libel was but one step away; and Christian clerics proceeded to create the calumny that, for Pesach, when four cups of wine were drunk, the Jews also required the blood of a Christian.

But from where did Jews derive its use and significance? We cannot answer this with any degree of certainty. That wine was plentiful in ancient Israel is clear from Talmudic sources. Indeed, one scholar has demonstrated that, at the end of the third century c.e., the price of a flagon of wine was the same as that of a loaf of bread, and that wine was much cheaper than honey or oil.[1] It was natural, therefore, that amid the regular toasts to their friends and families, the custom of "toasting" or blessing the Almighty should have developed, and that this should have become a natural accompaniment to all religious rituals.

Some scholars trace its origin to the wine libations in the Temple, though it is unlikely that the Temple authorities would have condoned the transference of a sacred Temple ritual to an external, albeit religious, context. We would have to assume, therefore, that its use as a sacred draught originated during the period of the Babylonian captivity (post-586 B.C.E.), when the Temple was in ruins, with no prospects of its being rebuilt. It may have been introduced at that time as part of prayers for the restoration and as a nostalgic reminiscence.

Some view its origin as a borrowing from upper-class Hellenistic banqueting practice. Professor S. Stein has described the origin of the Haggadah as emanating from the Greek "Symposia literature," where entertainment, consisting of music, dance, and dramatic readings was provided. The Haggadah was a Jewish version of the Symposia compositions. Now, at the conclusion of those banquets, and as a prelude to the entertainment, wine was poured out in honor of the Greek gods. The four cups, it is suggested, may have been part of that same borrowing, but not until the Sages had prescribed a blessing over wine—*Borei periy ha-gafen*—

in order totally to purge the ritual of any idolatrous association and to invest it with holy significance.

We know that wine was part of the formality of the dining rituals of the Qumran Covenanters, for there is a regulation in their *Serach Ha-Yachad* ("Rules of the Community") that, "When they assemble at table to eat or to take wine, the priest shall stretch forth his hand first to bless the bread or the wine."[2] It is possible, therefore, that its sacred use began with the sectarians, from which it was taken into mainstream Judaism.

The drinking of four cups of wine became, over the centuries, the predominant motif of the Seder, over-shadowing the other rituals of *matzah* and *maror*, even though the four cups are purely a rabbinical require-ment and the others are biblical. Indeed, in the 15-word Order of Contents, recited aloud at the commencement of the Seder, there is mention of *Kiddush* (the first of the four cups), but no reference to "the four cups." This might have been in order to keep to a total of fifteen words, a liturgically significant number. Nevertheless, as the four cups are, arguably, more important than *Urechatz*, wherein only the Seder leader washes his hands (before handling the vegetables), or than *Nirtzah*, a term that does not denote any ritual, and is not even found in the composition *Chasal Siddur Pesach* with which it is associated, one might have assumed that a place for "the four cups" would have been found in that Order of Contents in preference to the latter two.

Its absence from that list is truly mystifying, espe-cially in the light of the centrality of that particular ritual. Indeed, it appeared as the central motif in several early printed editions of the Haggadah. In 1512, a Latin translation of the Haggadah was produced, directed at a Christian readership, in order to refute the virulently anti-Semitic propaganda of Johannes Pfefferkorn, an apostate who put himself under the protection of the Dominican monks who encouraged him to write, and published, several of his vituperative anti-Jewish tracts, particularly aimed at discrediting the Talmud. On the cover of this volume, written to prove that there were neither anti-Christian references nor any ritual requiring, or even obliquely referring to, Christian blood, anywhere in its pages, the cover of the book depicts Jews seated around a festive table. In order to signal that this is a Seder table, four cups are placed in front of each place.

Interestingly, this motif of the four cups, though slightly adapted, has been used by the Israeli wine producers, Carmel Mizrachi, on their publicity material. They show a Seder table depicting four "types" of wine: An aperitif for before the meal; a glass of white wine for the fish; a glass of red wine for the meat course; and a glass of sweet wine to follow the meal.

It matters not how far from tradition a family or group is, they will still zealously maintain the four cups requirement. Hence, it remained an obligatory and meaningful ritual within the format of the many Haggadot published by the secular Kibbutz movement this century, most of which diverged widely from the traditional text, replacing it with a whole variety of readings and adaptations.

There is a debate as to whether or not, at the outset, there was an obligation on each person to drink the four cups or whether it was merely an essential element in the Seder proceedings, to the extent that, provided that one person (or more) shared in the consumption of four cups, the requirement was fulfilled.

Protagonists of the latter view refer to the Mishnah in *Pesachim* (ch. 10), which seems to refer exclusively to the Seder leader partaking of the four cups among his other administrative duties:

> *They pour out for him the first cup (10:1) . . . They bring before him a variety of vegetables (10:2) . . . They pour out for him the second cup (10:4) . . . They pour out for him the third cup (10:7).*

The idea is that the Seder leader should display tokens of freedom, and the other members of the family should facilitate that image by acting out the role of his attendants.

The Mishnah also seems to make the Seder recitations (other than the Four Questions) the sole task of the one leading the Seder. Hence, the singular pronoun is employed throughout the description, unlike the normal Mishnaic convention, which is to employ the plural participial form, as in the very opening Mishnah: *Me'eimatai kor'in et Shema* ("From when may *one* (literally, 'they') read the Shema in the evening." Significantly, however, throughout that Mishnaic description of the Seder in Temple times, we find the singular form:

> He *commences by uttering verses of deprecation* [*of our ancestors*], *and* he *concludes with expressions of*

praise . . . until he *has concluded the entire chapter (10:4) . . . Until where (in Hallel) does* he *recite? . . . And* he *concludes with the blessing of Redemption (10:6). Over the fourth cup* he *concludes the Hallel and* he *recites over it the Blessing over the Song. Between the [first and last two] cups, if* he *wishes to drink further,* he *may; between the third and fourth* he *may not drink.*

The singular formulation suggests that both the recitation of the Haggadah as well as the drinking of the four cups was left to the one leading the Seder, usually the father, whose major role was to generate curiosity, initiate discussion, and inspire his son with nationalistic attachment to his people, their fate, and their destiny.

Another piece of evidence that it was the Seder leader alone who drank the four cups is that same Mishnah's reference to the duty of the authorities "to provide not less than four cups even for the poor man who is fed from the communal welfare kitchen" (10:1). If it was incumbent upon all the members of the family, gathered around the Seder tables, to drink four cups, then one might have expected the Mishnah to have insisted that the welfare administrators provide not just for the poor man, but for every member of his family.

It is because we assume that the *Arba' kosot,* the four cups we drink as part of the Seder ritual, are essentially one integrated *mitzvah* that we may be surprised at the suggestion that originally it was the Seder leader alone who drank. In truth, however, "each cup stands as an independent *mitzvah*"[3] (109b), with its own specific ritual purpose within the overall scheme and structure of the Haggadah.

The first cup is for *Kiddush*, and the third cup is over Grace after Meals. These are not unique to the Seder, since they are also part of the regular Shabbat and festival celebrations. It is thus only two of the cups that are Seder specific; and no additional halachic significance accrues as a result of their combination or as a result of the collective name of "four cups" that attaches to them.

Just like the "four species" of Sukkot, the "four cups" became synthesised into one unit, and regarded as one single *mitzvah*, a concept that was reinforced by the symbolic interpretations that were given to them. Thus, they were conceived as representative of the four expressions of redemption in Exodus 6:6–7; or of the four times the word *cup* is mentioned in the episode of Pharaoh's butler's dream (Genesis 40:11–13), which facilitated the meteoric rise of Joseph to power and influence in Egypt; or of the four kingdoms that subjugated Israel—the Assyrians, Persians, Greeks and Romans—and of the cups of retribution that God will ultimately give to drink to the nations that oppress Israel.

These interpretations, which artificially welded the four cups into a single, integrated, ritual *mitzvah*, raised halachic problems, such as why no blessing was prescribed over that unified *mitzvah* of drinking "the four cups"? A formula such as *Barukh attah . . . asher kids-*

hanu bemitzvotav vetzivanu al arba' kosot might have been expected.

David Abudraham explains that no blessing was prescribed precisely for the reason we have explained, namely that they should not be viewed as a single *mitzvah*-unit since each cup has its own specific, and separate, ritual purpose[4] (*Avudraham Ha-Shalem*, p. 215). Another distinguished halachist, the author of *Or Zaru'a* believes, however, that a blessing might well have been prescribed over the four cups, were it not that they were all separated and interrupted by readings, the meal, conversations, and so on, and we only make a blessing over mitzvot that are performed at one time.

Thus, it seems that a development in practice took place over the ages, from the original situation of there being a Seder leader, with the rest of the family acting as facilitators of the enacted religious drama, to a later situation wherein everyone present was an active participant, reading the Haggadah for themselves, together with the leader, and drinking four cups of wine for themselves.

The surprising omission of any reference to the four cups in the introductory Contents formula, *Kaddesh Urchatz*, may also reflect that same development that has taken place as regards this ritual, and the fact that it was not originally incumbent upon all the participants at the Seder.[5] (*Urchatz*)

NOTES

1. D. Sperber, Roman Palestine, 200–400: Money and Prices (Ramat Gan, Bar Ilan University, 1991), p. 115.

2. M. Burroughs, *The Dead Sea Scrolls* (London, Secker & Warburg, 1956) p. 378.

3. Tal. *Pesachim* 109b.

4. See Avudraham Ha-Shalem (Jerusalem, Usha Publishing Co., 1963), p. 215.

5. The same may be said, of course, for *Urchatz*, which is included in the introductory Contents notwithstanding the fact that it is only the Seder leader who washes his hands at that early stage! Its inclusion, however, may well have been merely to help make up the significant total number of fifteen Contents entries. Its lesser importance in that list is indicated by the fact that it does not stand on its own as a separate entry, but is merely tacked on to the opening word *Kaddesh* by means of the conjunctive *vav* (*Urchatz*).

9

ॐ

Four Sons or One?

Shakespeare wrote of the seven ages of man. They are all separate and independent stages of human development, and the way we relate to each of them is totally different, marking us out as having not one, but seven, totally different lives. We go through those seven experiences, conditioning ourselves for, and, in turn, being conditioned by, the challenges, problems, and trials we encounter, by the strength or weakness of will we possess at each of those times to meet those challenges, as well as by the nature and scope of our ambitions and expectations of life at each of those stages. Shakespeare knew it so well:

All the world's a stage, and all the men and women
    merely players.

They have their exits and their entrances.
And one man in his time plays many parts,
His acts being seven ages.

(*As You like It*, ii. 7)

Each of us lives out seven variant, concurrent lives, with each melding seamlessly, we hope, into its succeeding age and stage. Most of us will probably find some of the stages or ages more pleasurable than others. The fear and uncertainty experienced by "the infant, mewling and puking in the nurse's arms," not knowing whether his creature comforts will be attended to promptly or at all, may, for all we know, be as, or more, traumatic than those of "second childishness and mere oblivion—sans teeth, sans eyes, sans taste, sans everything."

If life has any purpose or benefit, we are truly in a state of constant growth and change. And unless we live on a desert island, interacting with no one and adjusting to no changing circumstance, we will truly live out our years as seven different people, with all the attendant opportunity that that offers: notably the ability to compensate in one age for the potential that we squandered in another.

On Succot we encounter the same concept amid the midrashic symbolism of the Four Species, each representing a different type of Jew: One, like the *etrog*, with taste and bouquet, Torah learning, and good deeds; another like the *lulav*, the palm, with taste but no bouquet, learning unaccompanied by good deeds; the third, like the myrtle, with bouquet but no taste, good deeds, though not predicated on Jewish values; and the last type, like the willow, with neither taste nor bouquet, neither knowledge of his religion nor good deeds.

The diversity of this heterogeneous group is recognized in this midrash, and regarded as a strength rather than a weakness. Hence the fact that those four diverse species are all bound together as one, with a single blessing made over them all, as if to acknowledge, accord respect, and even *thank* God for each and every group, including the last.

This is also how we might understand the four sons of the Haggadah: as paralleling the four Jewish "types" symbolized by the Four Species, on the one hand, combined with Shakespeare's notion of the single life divided up into totally variant ages and stages, on the other.

We would thus be looking not at four separate sons, but at a single son whose attitudes and relationships with Judaism's teachings vary greatly at different times of his life, often as a result of the changing circumstances and strains and stresses of his life, the moral dilemmas he cannot resolve, the temptations into which he is drawn, and the personal misfortunes that challenge his faith and seem to refute his inherited traditions.

We try and ensure that all our children grow up in the *chakham*, mold, with a good Jewish education. And we assume that this will necessarily give them a moral and spiritual basis for the rest of their lives. But "it ain't necessarily so!" For, in the words of *Pirkei Avot*, "Whoever does not add, subtracts." So the young *chakham*, so enthusiastic and involved with his Judaism as a child, often grows up into adolescence, finding no time for his religious practice or his learning, and, instead, embracing the values of the *rasha*, leading a rejectionist way of life.

But that adolescent *rasha* soon matures, and on finding that the cults and kicks of a superficial teenage culture have lost their appeal, he or she comes to realize that there *has* to be more to life than physical gratification and leisure pursuit. And so they commence on a tentative search for meaningful and timeless values.

It is at that point, when they have returned to the starting line of a long and demanding return to faith and knowledge, that some join the ranks of the *tam*, the simple son, prepared to admit their ignorance, to ask *Mah zot*, "What is this?" willing to ask for guidance and clarification at every turn, no matter how simple and naive they know their question might be.

There are others, however, who, while acknowledging the emptiness of their current lives, yet cannot summon the will to make the many sacrifices that they know a return to a full Jewish life will involve. Their lethargy places them squarely in the ranks of the *eino yode'a lish'ol*, those who have no questions to ask; those who stand back, not wanting to be influenced, not wishing to confront the difficult questions of who they are, what is their relationship with their people, what is going to bind them together as a family, what sort of culture is going to win the battle for their, and their children's, soul, mind and emotions.

But it goes further: For once we understand the Four Sons as four stages and levels of an individual's dialogue with faith, then we have to note that they do not always follow chronologically, with age and maturity. Sometimes they represent simultaneous facets of the makeup of a single individual.

We have all encountered the *chakham*, the wise man, even the scholar or religious leader, who is yet, at the same time, a *rasha*. The man whose Torah and scholarship is all theoretical. The mind without a conscience to go with it. The brilliant theorist who divorces practice from principle, essence from form, morality from ritual.

We have all encountered people who are clearly *chakham*, intelligent and educated, and yet who, in certain respects, view life from the perspective of the *tam*, the simple son, wholly impractical, naive and thoughtless when it comes to relationships with spouses, children, family, or friends.

And we have all encountered supposedly wise people who are also *eino yode'a lish'ol*, who think that they know it all, and who regard it as a weakness to ask questions, to share their problems, to seek advice or help from others, and who end up plunging themselves and their families into difficulties or debt.

We all vacillate between any one, or more, of those four character traits at any particular time of our lives. We are rarely possessed of just one trait, to the exclusion of the others.

And that is why none of us can be smug, whatever our level of wealth or achievement in life, whatever our level of religious or secular knowledge, whatever our level of observance. And none of us should seek, therefore, to marginalize or delegitimize those in a different category.

Kneged arba'ah vanim dibrah Torah, "The Torah speaks of four levels of relationship and identification with our heritage." We cannot be sure that we will feel the same next year about our heritage, our community, or even ourselves, as we feel at this moment. We are all in an inexorable process of change, of searching for the attainable as well as for the elusive, for meaning and permanence, for truth and trust, for pleasure that is a state of mind rather than a transient fix, for the here and the hereafter, as well as for the things that are dressed up as those values but whose inner core is emptiness and void. But the Torah addresses us all, at whatever point of existential perplexity we may be. *Dibra Torah*: The Torah speaks to us, and offers us guidance and support, to find the true elixir of life and life eternal.

The Son Without Questions

The motif of "The Four Sons" derives from the fact that in four passages of the Torah reference is made to questions that our children will pose in the future. The rabbis assumed, therefore, that each question was representative of a particular level of religious orientation or degree of intellectual sophistication.

But there appears to have been some dispute among those early authorities as to the precise attribution of those biblical verses. Thus we find a difference of opinion between the consensus midrashic view, on the one hand, and the author of the Haggadah, on the other, regarding which son Exodus 13:8 refers to. The verse reads, "And you shall tell your son in that day, saying: 'It is on account of all the Lord did for me (liy) when I came out of Egypt,'" and the Midrash attributes this to the son without questions (*eino yode'a lish'ol*). Hence *Rashi*'s comment on that verse: "The Torah teaches us here that we have a duty to open up the child who does not ask questions by means of legends that will excite his imagination." And yet, as anyone who has ever paid attention to the reading of the Haggadah will know, this is the very proof text that is employed here as the verse with which to harry the *rasha'*, the wicked son! Indeed, we make great play of emphasizing the word *liy*, "for me," in order to exclude the *rasha'* from the fraternity of the redeemed, or those worthy of redemption ("*For me* God did all those things—but not for *him*. Had *he* been in Egypt, he would never have been redeemed!"). How then do we explain this variant attribution of the identical biblical verse?

We must assume that the author of the Haggadah was not ignorant of the rabbinic consensus that attributed that verse to the *Rasha'*, but that he wished to make a telling point by merging the identities of the *rasha'* and the *eino yode'a lish'ol* in this subtle way. He seems to be telling us that one who has no questions to ask about his heritage and his faith is on the road to becoming a *rasha'*. Indeed, this point is boldly enunciated in the maxim of *Pirkei Avot: Ein bor y'rei chet*, "An ignorant man cannot be God-fearing"[1] (*Pirkei Avot* 2:6). This means, in effect, that there is no neutrality in religious education. Not to give one's child a proper Jewish education means to educate him towards rejection. Not to excite his curiosity about his history and destiny, not to stimulate him to ask his questions and air his doubts, is to create not merely an *eino yode'a* lish'ol, a son without questions, but, ultimately, a *rasha'*, a renegade.

He is reminding us that a spiritual vacuum is not a neutral, but an adversarial, position, and that one cannot leave a child to "make up its own mind" about whether or not it wishes to lead a religious or moral life. For if that child is starved of true spiritual nourishment and deep knowledge, it can never be a free agent—a mere *eino yode'a lish'ol*. It must inevitably choose the easy option, the religiously undisciplined and morally lax option of society at large, and become, in religious terms, a *rasha'*.

This point is graphically made in the rabbinic comment regarding the pit into which Joseph was slung: We are told, *Vehabor reik ein bo mayim*, "The pit was empty; there was no water in it" (Genesis 37:24). But the rabbis could not accept that a pit is entirely "empty." Nature abhors a vacuum, and hence their comment: *Mayim ein bo aval nechashim v'akrabim yesh bo*, "There may have been no water in it, but snakes and scorpions there certainly were."[2] (Tal. *Shabbat* 22a)

The author of the Haggadah similarly espoused this view that one cannot have a spiritual or intellectual vacuum. If one is an *eino yode'a lish'ol*, if there is a vacuum in one's religious emotions and intellectual sensitivities, to the extent that one is totally unmotivated to ask questions, then that vacuum will be filled by thoughts, fantasies, sensations, plans, and ultimately actions, that are not merely non-religious, but anti-religious. The *rasha'* and the *eino yode'a lish'ol* are worthy bedfellows.

Parents have the solemn responsibility to ensure that their children's early enthusiasm is properly focused and constructively channeled. The four sons are, of course, categories, and refer, therefore, just as much to parents as to children. Parents have to strive positively to attain to the *chakham* category if they wish to raise their children accordingly. But if the parents are representative of the *eino yode'a lish'ol* grouping, if they do not constantly engage their children religiously, showing sincere interest in their Jewish education and nourishing thereby their Jewish identity, then they should not be surprised if one day, God forbid, their child opts for the *rasha'* category.

It has been appositely observed that the Hebrew numerical value (*gematria*) of the word *adam*, "man," adds up to 45. This is the same numerical value of the Hebrew word *mah*, meaning "what?" The implication is that when we cease to ask questions we squander our unique intellectual and moral curiosity and sensitivity.

So the motif of "The Four Sons" is aimed specifically at the one category of parent who can still do something to affect their children's spiritual growth: the parents of the child who is currently unmotivated, who has not yet been switched on to Judaism, to pride in, and knowledge of, his heritage, namely the *eino yode'a lish'ol*, the son without questions.

The parents of the *chakham*, the wise son, have no need to worry. The parents of the *rasha'* have already lost the opportunity. The parents of the *tam*, the child with limited intelligence, cannot reasonably expect great spiritual attainment. It is the parents of the child who simply has no questions to ask because his religious curiosity has not been aroused by dynamic teachers and keen and supportive parents: They are the ones to whom the passage of "The Four Sons" especially addresses its message.

NOTES

1. *Pirkei Avot* 2:6.
2. Tal. *Shabbat* 22a.

11

౨ఌ

Dislodging the Wicked Son's Teeth

The *Barukh Ha-makom* composition of the Passover Haggadah speaks in praise of God who "gave the Torah to *his people, Israel.*" The ensuing enumeration of the Four Sons is, in effect, an amplification of the term "his people, Israel." It asserts that Israel is not a monolithic or homogeneous entity, but is composed of groups of people with differing levels of knowledge and perception and varying degrees of spiritual commitment. And we have to inspire each of these groups to declare: *Barukh ha-makom*, "blessed be God."

This point is underlined by the fact that the four sons include the *rasha'*, the wicked one. He is also an object of divine concern; and the redemption from Egypt, and all subsequent redemptions, would be incomplete without him.

From this perspective, the Haggadist's treatment of the *rasha'* is mystifying:

What does the wicked son say? "What does all this ritual mean to you?" "To you" *(he says) but he does not include himself. And since he has excluded himself from the community and denied the existence of God,* you also may dislodge his teeth (hak'heh et shinnav) *and tell him: "It is on account of what the Lord did* for me *when I went out of Egypt." "For me" (you should stress), but not* for him. *Had he been there, he would not have been redeemed!*

Not only the brusque reply that the father is recommended to make to the *rasha'*, but particularly the violent act of "dislodging his teeth," seem totally incompatible with Judaism's tolerant tradition.

Most commentators, however, explain the Hebrew phrase *hak'heh et shinnav* in the metaphorical sense of "blunt his teeth"; that is, "stifle his argument," "parry his challenge," by the sting of your sarcastic response. Indeed, in this sense the phrase is applied in several midrashic passages.[1]

As we cannot date the passage in our Haggadah with any degree of precision, we cannot know whether or not the phrase had already taken on that metaphorical usage by the time our Haggadist employed it. It is therefore equally possible that it is actually being employed in the literal sense of dislodging or loosening the teeth of the *rasha'* by means of a violent blow! On this hypothesis, we may ask how such an uncharacteristic reaction can possibly be recommended in the context of a passage that sets out to include the *rasha'* among the Four Sons who are *all* deserving of the Torah's sympathetic attention and for all of whom we declare: *Barukh ha-makom,* "Blessed be God." As a supplementary, we query the phrase *ve'af attah,* "And *even you* (may dislodge his teeth)"—a rather mystifying emphasis that calls for elucidation.

Now, the dialogue between the wicked son and his parent (or teacher[2]) is presented at two levels. All the biblical questions attributed to the various sons are presumed to be those that would be asked by any future generation of the post-Exodus era. Hence the biblical formulations: "When your son will ask you *tomorrow*[3] saying . . ." (Ex. 13:14; Deut. 6:20), or, "And it shall come to pass when your children will say to you . . ." (Ex. 12:26), and so on. However, the answer, provided here for the *rasha',* projects the situation back to the Exodus period, or at least the period of the wandering in the desert. From the answer, "on account of what the Lord did *for me when I came out of Egypt . . . ,"* we may assume that the Torah has in mind a parent who had personally come out of Egypt and is currently living through the period of the wandering in the desert.

This parent has given birth to a wicked son in the desert, and he tells that son that "had he been in Egypt (a little while ago), he would not have been redeemed." A son who had so "separated himself from the Israelite community" would never have been allowed to participate in the Passover eve-of-Exodus ritual. He would have been categorized as a *ben nekhar*, "an estranged son" (Ex. 12:43).

We must not fall into the exegetical trap of confusing, and thereby synthesizing, the statement made to the *rasha'*—"on account of what the Lord did *for me* when I came out of Egypt"—with the totally independent exegesis that appears much later in the Haggadah: "In every generation a man should consider it as if he had personally gone out of Egypt, as it states 'On account of what the Lord did *for me* when I came out of Egypt.'" The latter is a quite separate and alternative exegetical inference from the one contained in our *rasha'* passage, which, though employing the same phrase ("what the Lord did *for me*"), yet does so ironically. The author of the *rasha'* passage is not thinking of the renegade who surfaces in every generation; he clearly has in mind the unfeeling offspring of an Israelite who had, quite literally, come out of Egypt.

But we need to define that rebellious son's notional status a little more precisely. Had he "still been in Egypt" he could not have been regarded as a Hebrew slave, since he has clearly "separated himself from the community." The only other category of slave our tradition recognizes is that of a Canaanite slave (*'eved kena'ani*). Ethnically this is most appropriate. Since the Hebrews in Egypt hailed from Canaan, one who divests himself of his exclusive Hebrew identity is left only with the nationality derived from his country of origin.

Now the Israelite father of that rebellious son, notwithstanding the need to admonish him sharply, is also reminded of the fact that the Torah speaks of four sons. The Torah demands that that son's wickedness be purged so that he may also be redeemed to join in his people's destiny. As a Canaanite slave, there is but one way that he could gain immediate freedom, and that is the manner described in Exodus 21:27: "And if the master *knocks out the tooth* of his manservant or maidservant, he shall let him go free on account of his tooth." This, we suggest, is the whole object of that *symbolic* dislodging of the wicked son's teeth, as alluded to by the phrase *hak'heh et shinav*. It is a ritual granting of manumission to one who, had his defection from the ranks of his people taken place during their slavery in Egypt, would never have secured his freedom at the Exodus.

One difficulty remains, however: The biblical law of manumission of the Canaanite slave refers to the master—not his father—knocking out his teeth! It is with this difficulty in mind, we suggest, that the Haggadist tells the father of that renegade son: "Even you *(ve'af attah)* may (symbolically) dislodge his teeth"—even though you are not his master.

But how is it that the father, himself a slave to the Egyptians, could possibly assume the role of master, to grant manumission to another slave? To answer this question we must turn to the book of Genesis, and the story of Noah's drunkenness. When Ham the father of Canaan looked on indifferently at his father's nakedness, Noah, on awakening, cursed his progeny thus: "Cursed be Canaan; a *servant of servants* he shall be to *his brethren*" (Gen. 9:25).

Thus, the Canaanites were destined to occupy the lowliest status of any nation. They alone may even become servants of servants, to the extent that the Israelites, servants to the Egyptians, could, in turn, regard the Canaanites as their own personal servants, with the concomitant duty of granting them their liberation if they inflict any loss of limb upon them.

Hence, the Israelites, in Egypt, and subsequently in the desert, were commanded to ensure the liberation of their entire nation, and the return to the fold of every one of their "four sons"; even those in the *rasha'* category who, by separating themselves from the community, had assumed the status of Canaanite slaves.

As a prelude to their repentant readmission to the community, the father administers a symbolic blow to the teeth, reminding the *rasha'*, at the same time, that his redemption is purely through the grace of the Torah law of manumission and not through any personal merit.

NOTES

1. See M. Jastrow, *Dictionary*, pp. 1321–1322.

2. "Sons" and "disciples" are synonymous in the rabbinic viewpoint. This is reflected in the well-known Talmudic statement that "whoever teaches his neighbor's child is considered as the latter's parent" (*San.* 19b).

3. That is, at any future time.

12

ৼ৸

"Not Just Once,
but in Every Generation . . ."

Pesach is the festival that gets to the heart of the Jewish condition. Thoughts about enslavement and redemption lead us effortlessly into consideration of the plight of our people, literally since the Egyptian era. It is almost impossible to think of what being a Jew means without reflecting on our pockmarked history. And in the modern era it is impossible to think Jewishly without marveling at our return to Zion, notwithstanding all the anguish attending that return.

One passage of the Haggadah, in particular, draws attention to the anomaly that the early Zionists used to refer to as "the Jewish problem": "For not just once, but in every generation they rose against us to destroy us, and the Holy One, blessed be He, saved us from their hands."

How uncannily and tragically prescient of those sages, some 2000 years ago—before the notion of blind anti-Semitism was ever conceived—to have foreseen all that, and incorporated it into the Haggadah. How could they possibly have known that, literally, "in every generation," Jews were going to be singled out as objects of ridicule and victims of discrimination, persecution, violence, and ultimately, genocide?

They were not prophets. They made no claim to that. Indeed, they asserted that the age of prophecy was long over with the passing of Haggai, Zechariah, and Malachi, the last of the biblical prophets. But they were sages, men who were capable of isolating the core ethical and moral imperative to which Jews had to respond as long as they wished to remain true to their heritage. They knew, therefore, that Jews, of necessity and instinctively would pit themselves against the forces or evil and oppression, whenever and wherever those ugly forces manifested themselves in the world.

Their first father, Abraham, had stood *contra mundum*, pitching himself into a violent battle involving nine kings of the east, a battle over an issue that was of no consequence to him, simply because he saw that as his chance to rescue his nephew, Lot, who had been taken prisoner by one coalition. So the descendants of Abraham would find themselves, "in every generation," affronted, outraged, and compromised by such forces of evil and brutality attempting to overwhelm the weak and the defenseless. In response to that, the sages of the Haggadah knew, Jews would, likewise, feel constrained to pitch themselves into the fray as champions of truth, peace, and righteousness, which would, inevitably and inexorably, lead to our people being resented and oppressed "in every generation."

And just as those ancient sages foresaw that their descendants would not flinch from their duty, so they were convinced that, with justice on their side, "the Holy One, blessed be He, would save them from their hands."

There is a supreme irony that, having survived, by the skin of our teeth, the millennial battles and pogroms launched against us by the other nations, our people in Israel should today find themselves so bitterly divided, with enflamed feelings of antipathy between the religious and the secular, Ashkenazim and Sephardim, black Jews and white Jews, the political right and the left, and all those together in concert against the vast influx of new immigrants.

We should pray not only for the remnant of our brethren who remain behind, in straightened circumstances, in the countries of the former Soviet Union, and who suffer from the age-old antipathy of their Christian and Muslim fellow citizens, but also for our brethren in the State of Israel—fortunate beneficiaries of a modern-day liberation. Too many of them continue to harbor an antipathy that was hitherto regarded as the exclusive hallmark of the anti-Semite, but which now seems to have attached itself to us as a legacy of shame that we must strive to disown.

CHAPTER
13

و

R. Eleazar's Dispute with the Sages

There is a halachic piece of exegesis, which is found in the Talmud[1] and reproduced in the Pesach Haggadah,[2] which, because of its abstruseness for the non-talmudist, is generally gabbled through with no attempt to discover its import.

I refer to the discussion on the verse, *Lema'an tizkor et yom tzeitkha me'eretz mitzrayim kol yemei chayyekha*, "in order that you shall remember the day you went out of Egypt all the days of your life" (Deuteronomy 16:3), from which Ben Zoma inferred that the third paragraph of the *Shema*, dealing with the Exodus, was to be included in the nighttime recitation of that prayer, and from which the sages, employing the identical exegetical method, made a totally different inference.

Both disputants based their inferences on the assumption that there was no superfluous word in the Torah, and if there did appear to be one, then it was placed there in order to convey an extension of the contextual meaning. Now, it would have been sufficient for the Torah to have told us that we must remember the day we went out of Egypt: *yemei chayyekha* "each day of your life." The additional word *KOL* (*yemei chayyekha*), "ALL (the days of your life)," for Ben Zoma, comes to include the nights as well. He understands *Kol yemei chayyekha* as, "[Let its recitation extend over] the *entire day* of your life, morning and night. The sages, however, while noting the superfluous word *kol*, yet believe it was put there for a different reason, namely to extend the recitation of that paragraph not merely to the period of man's normal earthly "days," but also to his glorious existence in the Messianic era.

Their respective views have been attributed to the fact that, since the Exodus proper did not occur until the morning of the fifteenth of Nisan, the sages saw no reason to recite that third paragraph of the *Shema*, with its reference to the Exodus, at night. Ben Zoma (and R. Eleazar ben Azariah), on the other hand, maintained that, since the permission to leave was granted at midnight, after the last plague struck, it was therefore only right that the third paragraph should be included in our night prayers. We will see, however, from the continuation of the account of this Talmudic dispute, that this is only a partial explanation and that the dispute goes much deeper.

The Talmud[3] proceeds to quote Ben Zoma as rebutting the view of the sages and challenging the proposition that in the Messianic era we shall still be referring to the Exodus from Egypt. He adduces the verse in Jeremiah: "Behold days will come, saith the Lord, when they shall no longer say: 'As the Lord liveth who brought the Children of Israel out of the land of Egypt'; but rather, 'As the Lord liveth who brought up and led the seed of the house of Israel out of the land of the north and from all the countries whither I had driven them'; and they shall dwell in their own land" (Jeremiah 23:7–8).

The sages' response is that Jeremiah did not really mean that all references to the Exodus would be expunged in the Messianic era, but that the *shibbud malkhuyyot*, the oppression at the hands of successive kingdoms would at that time be the *leitmotif* of our historical consciousness and liturgical reminiscence, and the reminiscences of the Exodus from Egypt would be subsidiary. The parallel offered by the Talmud is the reference to Jacob's name change, where God said, *Lo yikkarei shimkha o'd yaakov kiy im yisrael yih'yeh sh'mekha*, "Your name shall no longer be called Jacob, but Israel shall be thy name" (Genesis 35:10), whereas even four verses later we find him still being referred to as Jacob. The Talmud avers that the same principle is to be applied: "Not that the name Jacob will be henceforth expunged, but that Israel will be the main name and Jacob the subsidiary."

In the ensuing Talmudic discussion of this issue,[4] the notion of greater trials displacing earlier ones in the nation's consciousness is buttressed by the following quotation: " Remember not the former things, neither consider the latter ones. For I shall perform a new thing; now shall it spring forth" (Isaiah 43:18–19). This is expounded to refer to the circumstances attending the wars of Gog and Magog in the Messianic era, a period when references to both the Exodus and the *shibbud malkhuyyot* would both be displaced by that uniquely cataclysmic event. The parable is given of the wayfarer who is attacked by a wolf and escapes, and who constantly relates that particular episode until the day when he is attacked by a lion and again escapes. Then it is the story of the lion that he constantly relates, until the relating of both of those episodes is further displaced by his miraculous escape from the bite of a serpent. So it is with Israel, *Tzarot acharonot meshakchot et harishonot*, "the most recent tribulations cause the earlier ones to be forgotten."

This dispute between the sages and Ben Zoma is a trifle perplexing, however, since the illustration just quoted, and especially its concluding proverb, although ostensibly being marshalled as a support for the view of the sages—namely, that the Exodus will continue to be recounted in the Messianic era, albeit as a subsidiary concept—yet appears rather to weigh the scales in favor of the view of Ben Zoma! Note especially the reference in the proverb to "causing (the earlier tribulations) *to be forgotten.*"

Indeed, it is significant that, immediately before R. Eleazar ben Azariah's statement ("Behold I was like a man of seventy . . ."), the Mishnah states categorically

"We make mention of the Exodus at night."[5] This is presented as an anonymous statement—a ruling—with no opposing view quoted. This suggests that both R. Eleazar and Ben Zoma, as well as the sages, were, in fact, all in agreement that, in the context of the practical *halakhah* governing the developing liturgy, the Exodus was indeed to be included in the nighttime *Shema*. Their dispute centered rather on whether this was biblically mandated,[6] through the words of the *kol yemei chayyekha* verse (as Ben Zoma averred) or whether its recitation was rooted merely in rabbinic authority since the *kol yemei chayyekha* verse referred to a totally different time frame, namely the Messianic era (as expounded by the sages).

Thus, it is clear that the dispute between R. Eleazar ben Azariah and Ben Zoma, on the one side, and the sages on the other, had a far wider ramification. It would seem that the sages, in particular, by seeking biblical authority for the necessity of relating about the Exodus in the Messianic era, were seeking to widen the discussion to encompass the degree to which historical consciousness should be allowed to overshadow contemporary reality. The Sages seem to be suggesting that not only do we take the past with us into the future, but that the Jew is forever conditioned by, and inexorably reliving, his past history, and that the period up until and including the Messianic era will be a precise rerun of the conditions attending the Exodus. It follows then that we could not have expected the present *galut* (state of exile) of pre-Messianic Jewish history to be any less harsh than the *galut* in Egypt that preceded the Exodus.

That is, to a large extent, a pessimistic philosophy, and yet it is, of course, the reality of the past twenty centuries, as expressed so succinctly in the *Vehiy she'amda:* "For not only once did they stand up to destroy us, but in every generation they arise to destroy us." And, as far as the sages' parable is concerned, although we may cease to recount our escape from lesser dangers as more violent situations present themselves, yet the shadow of the Egyptian bondage, of a Pharaoh who set out to kill every Jewish male and seize the women—the shadow of genocide—will never vanish until the Messianic era. That, for the sages, is the primary implication of the phrase *kol yemei chayyekha.*

And this also explains the force of the word *lehaviy* (*liymot ha-mashi'ach*), "which means," literally, "*to bring to*" (the days of the Messiah), an expression that is not used by Ben Zoma in the course of his inference. He does not say *lehaviy haleilot*[7]. "To bring to" the Messianic era underscores the deeper level of meaning that the sages are highlighting, namely, that we bring with us to the Messianic era the "repetitive syndrome" of our Egyptian experience.

For Ben Zoma, however, the parable and its proverb are to be taken quite literally, and there will not remain even a subsidiary position to be allocated to the Exodus in Israel's national consciousness in the Messianic era. We will have cut all ties with our past, and the totally transforming experience of that post-historical transcendent moment will render all (our) past history unconnected and irrelevant. So unique and sublimely unimaginable will that time be that even Isaiah could only refer to it as "a new *thing*" that God would perform. It will defy description, since it will bear no relation to any other historical time. Indeed, so irrelevant is the very notion of time in relation to it that, Isaiah is telling us, if we must at all refer to it, we can only dub it a "thing" (43:19).

Rabbi Eleazar ben Azariah was one of the most brilliant and distinguished scholars of the Yavneh academy. The Mishnah itself records how, although only eighteen years of age on the day of his appointment as *Nasi*,[7] he was yet able to solve many halakhic problems that had hitherto remained unresolved, to the extent that an entire Talmudic tractate, *Eduyyot*, was compiled from his decisions on that occasion. Furthermore, in addition to his halakhic expertise, he was also regarded as an incomparable master of *Aggadah*, midrashic exegesis. So confident was he in that position that he did not flinch from chiding the illustrious R. Akivah that he should stick to complex halakhic matters and not indulge in *Aggadah!*[8] We might wonder, therefore, why such a master of the midrashic method found himself unable to provide some biblical verse to serve as a proof text for his view that the Exodus should be incorporated into the evening prayers. It is strange that he required the assistance of Ben Zoma who, if the truth be told, hardly offered his colleague anything outstandingly original here. Surely the word *kol (yemei chayyekha)*, employed by the sages as the basis of their Messianic inference, would at the same time have readily suggested itself as a superfluous word that was available as a basis for his own particular inference!

We may offer two explanations. The first is that the motivating principle of Eleazar's exegetical philosophy was that of *Dibra Torah kilshon b'nei adam*, that "the Torah speaks in the language of men,"[9] and that interpretations or exegetical applications should be close to the simple sense of the verse. Thus, the superimposition of a Messianic teaching onto a straightforward phrase may well have been unacceptable to him on that score.

But this does not explain why, given his record of challenging the greatest scholars of his day, he required the assistance of Ben Zoma in countering the Messianic interpretation of the sages. We suggest that, as a young scholar, he might well have felt reticent to argue Messianic speculation with the sages, among whom there might have been some who had immersed themselves for years in the *Ma'asei Breishit* and *Ma'asei Merkabah* mysticism of the age, subjects that were traditionally not entered into until a scholar had reached middle age. Eleazar found a most powerful ally, however, in Ben Zoma, who was acknowledged as such an illustrious sage that the Talmud states, "Whoever sees Ben Zoma in a dream can expect to be blessed with wisdom."[10] In addition, Ben Zoma was one of "the four who entered the orchard," that is the four colleagues (the others being Ben Azzai, Elisha ben Avuyah, and Rabbi Akivah) who became initiated into the most advanced mystical speculation.[11]

We can understand, then, why the young R. Eleazar would have preferred to use Ben Zoma as an ally and exegetical spokesman once the sages presumed to use the *kol yemei chayyekha* verse as a proof text for Messianic speculation. Eleazar required the help of a mystic of Ben Zoma's distinction, whose view would have been respected by all when he asserted that that particular verse had no Messianic point of reference in the context of mystical lore.

NOTES

1. Talmud *Berakhot* 12b.

2. Section commencing: *Amar Rabbi Eleazar ben Azariah harei anni k'ven shiv'im shanah.*

3. Talmud *Berakhot* 12b.

4. Talmud *Berakhot* 13a.

5. Mishnah *Berakhot* 1:5 (12b).

6. This is the view of *Raavad* (quoted in the *Chiddushei Ha-Rashba ad loc.*), who makes the point that "it is inconceivable that they did not recite the third paragraph of the *Shema* at night at that time, since that would mean that they did not recite the *Emet ve'emunah* blessing (intrinsically connected to the former). This would be in flagrant conflict with the mishnaic principle that 'in the evening one recites two blessings after the *Shema.'*"

7. Talmud *Berakhot* 28a. The Palestinian Talmud (*Berakhot* 1:6), on the other hand, takes the phrase "I was [like] a man of seventy years" literally.

8. Talmud *Sanhedrin* 38b.

9. Talmud *Kiddushin* 17b.

10. Talmud *Berakhot* 57b.

11. Talmud *Hagigah* 14b.

A Problem Verse in *Dayyenu*

The problem we wish to highlight in this chapter is presented by a familiar line in the *Dayyenu* composition of the Pesach Haggadah: *Illu kervanu lifney har Sinai velo' natan lanu et ha-Torah dayyenu*, "Had He brought us near unto Mount Sinai, but not given us the Torah, it would have sufficed."

The problem is that the first halves of all the other conditional clause lines in this composition stand in their own right as self-sufficient and intrinsically beneficial acts of favor. They each constitute an independent boon whose benefit could be enjoyed without the supplementary boon enumerated in the second half of the line. Our problem line above stands out, however, in that it offers nothing of value to Israel in the first half of the line. For what purpose could possibly have been served by "bringing us near unto Mount Sinai" if this was not to be accompanied by the "giving of the Torah?" Without Torah, Sinai was nothing more than a deserted mountain, of no consequence as a stopping place for Israel!

The answer we propose is that the popular translation, "Had He brought us near unto Mount Sinai," misses the true nuance. It should rather be rendered, "Had He brought us near [to Himself] in front of (*lifnei*) Mount Sinai." The emphasis now is not on the mountain, but rather on the verb *kervanu*. The verb *karav* frequently denotes a spiritual proximity and convergence, a personal revelation or self-disclosure of God's presence, a human absorption into the experience of divine communion.

This meaning can be illustrated by reference to one of our best-known liturgical psalms (148:14):

> *He has lifted up a horn for* His people (*va-yarem keren l'ammo*)
> *A praise for all* His saints (*tehillah lekhol chasidav*)
> *For Israel, a people* in close proximity (*livney yisra'el 'am kerovo*)

The parallelism will be seen to contain a progressive amplification of Israel's attributes, from *'Am* to *chasid* to *'am karov*. The latter term must clearly be a more intense and elevated degree of spiritual attainment than that of "saint," supporting the notion of *karov* (*kerovo*) as "absorption into the experience of divine communion."

The same verb, *karav*, is employed in connection with the episode of the daughters of Zelafchad: *Va-yakreiv mosheh 'et mishpatan Lifney 'adonay*, "And Moses *brought* their case *close* to God" (Num. 27:5). The sense here is of Moses repeating his original Sinaitic audience with God, when the rest of the law was disclosed to him. Moses, in this instance, again brings their case before the very bar of divine jurisdiction. The sense of the verb *karav* is thus of a judge hearing a plea *in chambers*, in the closest informal proximity.

The overtone of intimacy and self-disclosure contained in the usage of the verb *karav* also explains the employment of this root as a euphemism for sexual intercourse.[1] Again, the noun *kirvah*, in both its occurrences[2] clearly denotes the state of proximity to God. *Kirvat 'elokim liy tov* does not mean "approaching God is good unto me," but rather, "God's *proximity* is good unto me," in an objective genitive sense.

Moving from biblical to rabbinic usage, we find the above nuance of *karav* expressed in an even more popular and overt sense. This forms the pivot of a midrashic comment on the verse, "Happy are they whom thou choosest and bringest near *(u-tekarev)*."[3]

The Midrash[4] here draws a distinction between those whom God merely "chooses," and those whom He chooses and also "brings close" *(karav)*. The Patriarchs are quoted as examples of those whom God chose but did not have to bring near, because they were able to achieve this proximity as a result of their own spiritual efforts. Jethro and Rahab, on the other hand, were not chosen by God, but God did bring them near when they demonstrated their readiness for conversion to monotheism.

The comment of the *Etz Yoseph*, clarifying the distinction between "choosing" and "bringing near" in this context, is pertinent to our thesis:

> *"Choosing" means that man finds favor in God's eyes on account of his goodly qualities. The Patriarchs, Abraham, Isaac, and Jacob, possessed goodly qualities, but God did not initially bring them close to aid them in their goodliness. Rather they strengthened themselves (spiritually) to walk before God. Rahab and Jethro, on the other hand, were not chosen, for they were not (initially) possessed of goodly qualities. However, God "brought them near," arousing them by means of Moses and Joshua, respectively.*[5]

From this Midrash, as elucidated by the *Etz Yoseph*, it is clear that the verb *karav* connotes a divinely initiated act of touching the souls of certain individuals, such as Rahab and Jethro, who of their own accord might never have achieved the leap of perfect faith. It may also denote a divine augmentation of preexistent faith and strength of spiritual purpose (as in the case of the Patriarchs). In the former case, God may employ intermediaries (such as Moses and Joshua) to arouse and inspire the would-be convert.

Another midrashic passage, on the same theme, highlights this special sense of the verb *karav*, as bringing into divine proximity, especially as a prelude to spiritual conversion:

I brought *Jethro* near *(Ani Keravti . . .), and did not keep him far. You also, when a man comes to you to become converted, if his intention is purely in the name of heaven,* bring him close *and do not keep him at a distance. From here we learn that while a person rejects another with his left hand, he should (at the same time)* bring him close *with his right hand.*[6]

In line with this rabbinic usage of the verb *karav* is a perfect example from the Haggadah itself: "At first our forefathers were idolaters, but now God has brought us close *(kervanu)* to His service."

The conditional clause under consideration from the *Dayyenu* composition—*'illu kervanu lifney har Sinai*—now takes on a new dimension. It may now be rendered: "Had God made us experience a close personal revelation *(kervanu)* before Mount Sinai, without having given us the Torah, it would have sufficed." The presumption is that God could actually have raised Israel to the same high spiritual gradation without having given them a tangible, written Torah. He could have inspired them spiritually by His mere proximity; the revelatory experience alone could have engendered a permanent bond of religious fealty, as it did with the Patriarchs.[7]

The type of instantaneous conversion here contemplated is akin to that recorded as having occurred in the case of a number of biblical heroes. Saul, for example, "as he turned to leave Samuel, God gave him a new heart" (I Sam. 10:9). The effect of this was to transform, in an instant, a naive youth into a man endowed with the highest prophetic spirit (vv. 6, 10). The same sudden spiritual transformation endowed Samson with his power of strength (Jud. 14:6) and David with his regal quality (I Sam. 16:13).

The experience referred to was possibly a sudden flash of psychological self-revelation, a realization of hidden potential and spiritual sensibility. The trauma caused by the instantaneity of the revelation is described by the heathen prophet Balaam: "Who sees the vision of the almighty, fallen down and with opened eye." The latter phrase—in Hebrew, *shtum ha-'ayin*—is appositely rendered "opened of mental eye" by a modern lexicon.[8]

God could, accordingly, have made Israel undergo that same experience whose instantaneous effect would have been no less potent (and probably more so) than that which was achieved by handing over to them a written Torah, which took time to digest and assimilate. The Torah could have remained a *Torah sheb'lev*, an inner spiritual identification, with Israel no less committed. Truly, "had He brought us into *revelatory proximity (kervanu)* in front of Mount Sinai, without having given us the (written) Torah, it would have sufficed."

NOTES

1. Gen. 20:4; Lev. 18:6, 14, 19; Deut. 22:14 et al.

2. Is. 58:2; Ps. 73:28.

3. Ps. 65:5.

4. Mid. *Bemid Rabb.* 3:2.

5. *Loc. cit.*

6. *Mechilta Yitro* on Ex. 18:6.

7. This sense of the root *Karav* underlies the Talmudic phrase: *Karov bekhol miynei Kreivut*, "He is near with every manifestation of nearness" (Pal. Talmud, *Berakhot* 13a).

8. Brown, Driver, Briggs, *Hebrew and English Lexicon of the Old Testament* (Oxford, 1907), p. 1060.

CHAPTER

15

ح‏

Rabban Gamaliel Used to Say . . .

One of the most straightforward yet perplexing passages of the Haggadah is the statement by Rabban Gamaliel that "whoever does not recite these three things on Pesach has not fulfilled his duty: *Pesach, matzah,* and *maror."*

Gamaliel goes on to explain in simple terms the significance of those three ritual elements, but we are not told on what halakhic principle he bases his view. If he is right, then this is a *mitzvah* without precedence in any other religious context, for in the case of no other *mitzvah* is its fulfilment predicated on a prior explanation of its significance.

Even in the case of the *mitzvah* of dwelling in the Succah, where the Torah states *Lema'an yeid'u doroteikhem,* "That your generations *may know* that I settled the Children of Israel in booths (Lev. 23:43)," yet there is no *mitzvah* to ensure that those around our *succah* table are actually informed of the significance of their abode. So why is Rabban Gamaliel so insistent that without such a public explanation one does not even fulfil the *mitzvah* of *Pesach*, *matzah* and *maror*?

A number of answers have been suggested, though one, quoted in Daniel Goldschmidt's critical edition of the Haggadah, has a particular contemporary resonance.

> *The Rabban Gamaliel referred to here is most likely the grandson of Hillel, who lived in the most turbulent period, a few decades before the destruction of the Temple in the year 70 c.e. His Patriarchate coincided with the dramatic expansion of the new religion of Christianity, which was utilizing all of Judaism's rituals, but was superimposing upon them a new, Christological significance, particularly related to events in the life and death of its savior.*[1]

The Paschal lamb became a symbol of the one who was taken to the crucifixion as "the lamb of God." The *matzah* wafers represented, as they still do in the Church's Communion, his body; and the *maror* symbolizes the bitterness of the suffering he endured.

Alarmed by such ideas, Rabban Gamaliel introduced an unprecedented measure, namely the necessity of publicly explaining the precise and Orthodox reason for the obligation to eat these foods. This would have had the added purpose of isolating those early schismatics from the mainstream Judaean community that they were trying to infiltrate. For they could hardly join a traditional Seder, knowing that they would have to suppress their own symbolism, and indeed be called upon to affirm the traditional Jewish explanation of these foods.

We know from Talmudic sources that Rabban Gamaliel was most zealous to outlaw any sectarian or non-Orthodox propaganda, and hence he decreed that an unauthorized *Targum*, Aramaic translation of the book of Job, should be buried under the Temple foundations.[2] He clearly feared that it may have been tampered with, and made to yield sectarian theological interpretations. It is consistent with such an approach, therefore, that, given its new Christological slant, Gamaliel should have demanded of Seder leaders that they lay particular emphasis on, and recite aloud the Orthodox explanation of *Pesach*, *matzah*, and *maror*.

They say that history repeats itself. If so, it will come as no surprise that, two thousand years on, Christianity, especially in the United States, is once again being attracted to our Seder ritual and emphasizing its Christological significance, and that Jewish authorities are, *à la Gamaliel*, speaking out and writing in condemnation of what one journal, in a banner headline, has called the "Christianizing of the Passover Seder."

Writing in the *Shema* journal, Debra Nussbaum Cohen observes that:

> *Christians of every ethnicity hold* [*the Seder*] *dear, because, for them, it is an annual reenactment of their*

Lord's last supper. In the last decade, as scholarship and curiosity among Christians as to the Jewish roots of their faith has grown, so has their interest in the Seder as they try to relate to it as a pivotal religious experience of their own.

An unfortunate phenomenon has begun to take root in many Protestant churches. They have begun holding sedarim emptied out of their Jewish content, and that content has been replaced with Christological interpretations . . . [The Messianic Jews are particularly capitalizing on this] and their Southern California district leader, Tuvia Zaretsky, brings his interpretation of a Seder to about 35 churches a year, as do each of the other seven missionaries on his staff.

Every single aspect of the ritual is "baptized." The three *matzot* are made to represent the Trinity; the *Afikoman*, which is broken, hidden, and dramatically returned at the conclusion of the meal, is recast to represent their Lord, broken on the cross, hidden from view in the empty cave, and subsequently resurrected. The *matzah's* holes represent the puncture wounds of the cross, the wine is transfigured into his blood, the saltwater into—and here's the rub—the tears that we Jews will shed when we realize what we have perpetrated in killing our own Messiah!

Since the Second Vatican Council in 1965 completely transformed the Catholic church's attitude to Jews and Judaism, the practice of annual sedarim has become widespread in Catholic parishes and homes throughout the United States. And, in order to counter that Christianizing of the Seder, many Progressive rabbis either volunteer to conduct an authentic Seder for their local Catholic church or invite the priests and leaders of the local church to their own communal Seder.

Orthodox rabbis are, of course, deeply offended by what they perceive as a hostile takeover bid, so reminiscent of the early days of nascent Christianity, and are suspicious of the view that this process can be held in check by a process of fraternization and clarification.

Writing in the same issue, A. James Rudin observes that "every religious tradition and every faith must have the absolute right to define and to interpret its own unique rituals, liturgies, and festivals. For others to do this sacred task is to invite distortion, lack of authenticity, and even animus."[3]

We should not be flattered by Christianity's interest in our rituals. We have suffered two thousand years of oppression, forced conversion, bloodshed, and Holocaust as a result of being Christianity's obsession and primary target. As the rabbinic proverb has it, in relation to the bee: *Lo m'uvshakh v'lo miduvshakh,* "I wish neither your honey nor your sting."

Rabban Gamaliel points the way as to how to deal with this problem, namely to intensify our understanding of our own heritage; to insist that there was, and always will be, only one original and authentically Jewish symbolism underpinning our religious rituals; and that it flows from, and back again to, the very heart of our nation and our national Covenant with God.

Any attempt by another religion to purloin our

ritual and to recast it in its own image only underscores the spiritual poverty of that religion and betrays its underlying purpose: to displace Israel from its special pedestal as God's Chosen People, as teachers of His law and primary recipients of His Spirit.

"*Kol shelo omar sheloshah devarim eilu bapesach lo yatza yedei chovato*: Whoever does not affirm his religious heritage has not fulfilled his duty." With Jews and Judaism being assailed from the forces of Christian fundamentalism on the right, and assimilation on the left, we truly all have *a duty to fulfill*. It is the duty of ensuring our own survival as Jews and the survival, in its authentic form, of our religious heritage. It is also to combat our gross internal ignorance, caused by most youngsters ceasing to learn their Judaism once they start to prepare for their bar mitzvah, thereby making them prey to those well-informed sectarians who are desperate to capture a Jewish soul.

Pesach is the festival of knowledge, as well as freedom. The Haggadah holds out that great challenge of bringing into dialogue every one of our children. Implicit in Rabban Gamaliel's statement is the warning that if we fail to educate them, then we have not fulfilled our duty, either to them or to our faith.

That history repeats itself is a sad truism. The problems and concerns of the first century remain those of the twenty-first century. *Plus ça change, plus ce la même chose.*

Do we learn from history? Emphatically, no.

NOTES

1. D. Goldschmid, *The Passover Haggadah: Its Sources and History* (Jerusalem, Bialik Institute, 1960), p. 51.

2. Tal. Shabbat 115a.

3. *Op. cit.*, p. 6.

CHAPTER

16

کو

The Message of Hillel's Sandwich

I am going to do a terrible thing for an Orthodox rabbi. I am going to change a rabbinic statement in order to apply it to our changed conditions.

I refer to the well-known passage in the Haggadah: *Va'afilu kulanu chakhamim, kulanu nevonim, kulanu yod'im et hatorah* . . . "And even if we were all scholars, all men of intellectual attainment, all masters of the Torah, there would still be a *mitzvah* for us to relate the circumstances of the Exodus from Egypt."

This passage was written in the heady period of Talmudic scholarship in Eretz Yisrael, when the goal of every schoolchild was to be accepted into the very selective higher academies of Jewish learning. This situation is chronicled so vividly in the famous story of Hillel. As a young man, he had come to Israel from

Babylon to sit at the feet of the great giants of the spirit who headed the Talmudic colleges of the Holy Land.

In those days students had to pay a daily tuition fee. It was winter, and the young Hillel had spent his entire allowance. Without money, he was turned away from the door by the college security. His passion for learning was such, however, that nothing would stand in his way, so he climbed up to a first floor window ledge on the outside of the building, just adjacent to the dais from which the scholars gave their lectures. By pressing his ears against the window, he could just make out what was being said inside. He was so engrossed in that activity, and so transported into the world of Torah speculation, that he was totally oblivious to the snow that was falling thickly and covering his body. As a result of the cold, coupled with exhaustion through lack of food, he collapsed, and remained in that dangerous condition the whole night.

The next morning, when the scholars entered their lecture hall, they observed that no light seemed to be coming in from that first floor window. They then discerned a strange shape, and, on investigation, they discovered the frozen Hillel in a desperate condition. Fortunately, they managed to thaw him out and resuscitate him.[1] Not surprisingly, with such a passion for knowledge, Hillel went on to become the most illustrious scholar of the entire Talmudic period, one who shaped the evolution of halakhah as none before or after him.

We can easily appreciate, therefore, in such a rarefied intellectual climate, how the sages saw the need to assert that, however scholarly a person may be, however *au fait* he may be with all the Torah sources and oral traditions regarding the slavery and Exodus from Egypt, yet he should not imagine that the *mitzvah* of sitting around a dining table and discussing all that with his family at a fairly superficial level does not apply to him. No matter how Jewishly well informed a person might be, there is a specific *mitzvah* to discuss the Exodus, with whomever is within earshot, on this special night. Depth of study and profundity of insight are not the essence of this night's challenge. What is required, rather, is an emotional, national, and existential identification with what our ancestors experienced at the dawn of our history.

Now to my revision of the statement of the Haggadah. Ours is an age of widespread ignorance of Jewish learning, with so many celebrating the Seder merely as a glorified dinner party, with little attempt, or ability, to recite the Haggadah and to immerse themselves in its core experience. Perhaps now we should rather say, *va'afilu kulanu ammei ha'aretz, kulanu chasrei de'a* . . . "And even if we were all untutored and ignorant of Judaism . . . yet there is still a *mitzvah* for us to relate the circumstances of the Exodus from Egypt."

No one is so ignorant that they cannot relate, especially in the post-Holocaust era, to Jewish suffering. And no one should be so insensitive, especially in the era of modern Israel, that he or she cannot grasp the implications, challenges, and pitfalls of freedom.

Knowledge is only a small part of what is required. We can empathize deeply with the experience of the Holocaust even though we could not pinpoint Auschwitz or Belsen on the map, and even if we had never read a single book on the subject.

This is certainly the assumption of the compilers of the Haggadah, and especially of the author of the "Four Sons" passage, which insists that we dialogue with every level of Jewish knowledge and commitment. This also explains the superficially formulated *Mah Nishtanah*, which allows for the participation of the youngest child.

We may speculate that this is also the reason for the strange incorporation into the Seder ritual of the *Koreikh*, or "Hillel's Sandwich" of *matzah* and *maror*—a mere duplication of the two symbolic foods already consumed! The Haggadah tells us that "this is what Hillel used to do: he would wrap together *matzah* and *maror* and eat them both (with the Paschal Lamb) in accordance with the biblical instruction . . ." Surely we would hardly have expected Hillel to do otherwise than follow the biblical instruction! Furthermore, why single out Hillel? Surely everyone else living, like him, in the period when the second Temple was still standing, also ate the Paschal Lamb together with *matzah* and *maror*, as biblically mandated?

The fact is that the Haggadah did not attain its final form until long after the destruction of the Temple, so there was truly no purpose served in including *Koreikh*—a second eating of *matzah* and *maror*—to recall the pre-destruction situation. Furthermore, the way we nostalgically recall that Temple practice is most unsatisfactory since we are partaking of but two out of the three foods that Hillel and his generation ate at one and the same time. They ate the Paschal Lamb, which we are prohibited from including as a symbolic food. So what was the whole point then, in attaching the name of Hillel to a practice that was universal from the time of the very first Seder in Egypt, and in recalling that practice in an inaccurate way that omits a basic component and is, at the same time, ritually repetitive?

We may speculate that the (post-destruction) compilers of the Haggadah had a great desire to incorporate a reference to the great Hillel, for nationalistic, social, and educational reasons. Hillel was a Babylonian who had risen to become the Patriarch of Israel. As such, he symbolized the unity of Israel and the Diaspora. He also traced his ancestry directly to the house of David, and thus represented a potent symbol of Jewish hopes for the restoration of their independence, hopes that received their most vigorous and urgent expression on Seder night. Hillel was also famous as the arch symbol of tolerance, and many examples of that are preserved in the Talmud. He practiced what his colleague Shammai merely preached, that we must "receive all men with a friendly countenance."[2]

Hillel made no distinction between great and small, learned or ignorant, observant or lax. He loved every Jew, and he would have been just as happy to have the wicked son as the wise one at his Seder. He would certainly have advised Jews not to underestimate their natural and deep-seated attachment to their history, and he also would have reassured them that that was not the exclusive preserve of the learned.

Hillel taught us that many who are ignorant of the "facts" of their history are, nevertheless, powerfully connected to the "fact" of their history. If they are but prepared to substitute a Jewish consciousness for a self-consciousness, they will readily rediscover Judaism as a rich provider of contentment and a sense of identity, and of a value system that delivers meaning, direction, and inspiration for their own and their family life.

The particular ritual associated with Hillel's name may not have been novel, but the mere mention of his name at the Seder conjures up principles of unity and tolerance without which the freedom we have so desperately prayed and fought for down the ages will continue to elude us. The Seder experience offers us but a foretaste of that freedom. The banquet is yet to come.

NOTES

1. Tamud *Yoma 35b*.
2. Mishnah *Avot* 1:15.

The Spirit of the *Shirah*

Imagine the feelings of the Israelites at that moment of destiny, as they gazed upon the carnage that had been wreaked upon their oppressors and surveyed the floating wreckage of Egyptian chariots, the flotsam of swords, javelins, and shields, the limp carcasses of thoroughbred stallions bobbing up and down, doing a dance macabre to the rhythm of the waves.

It is not difficult to guess what their instinctive reaction would have been. Any horde of suppressed, suffering, silenced slaves, suddenly granted the sight of their bitterest foes massacred in an instant, undoubtedly would have found themselves gripped by a mass hysteria. It would have prompted them to shout and scream, rave incoherently, hurl derision and abuse in the direction of their hapless victims, mocking their fate in the most intemperate manner and hailing their own prowess and achievement in having lured their enemies into such a masterly natural ambush.

We can appreciate, therefore, that one of the most characteristic and amazing aspects of the Israelites' reaction to the drowning of the Egyptians in the Red Sea was the calm and temperate, dignified and subdued way in which they accepted victory and deliverance:

> And Israel saw the great hand which God had exercised against Egypt. And Israel saw the Egyptians dead along the sea shore. And the people feared the Lord and they believed in God and in Moses his servant. (Exodus 15:31)

Their first reaction is one of heightened faith, not of personal or national vainglory. They instinctively thought of those who had made their victory possible: God and Moses. They remained contemplative, clear thinking, calm, and disciplined at a time when other victorious armies throughout history gave themselves up to the most riotous and frenzied forms of release and celebration.

Even their victory song was, in more ways than one, "composed." They were not permitted to give expression to their own independent feelings, which many might have framed through inappropriate slogans. It was the exclusive prerogative of Moses to recite each phrase of the poem of praise, after which the Israelites uttered the identical sentiment responsively.

This also ensured that their national reaction was a dignified and superbly moderated expression of joy and gratitude that their long ordeal was over and that God's greatness had been vindicated and venerated. True, there are references in it to the proud boasting of the Egyptians as they pursued the Hebrews: "I will pursue, I will overtake; I will divide the spoil. My desire shall be satisfied. I shall draw my sword; my hand shall dispossess them" (v. 9).

It does, indeed, refer to the ultimate fate of the foe in their watery grave: "You blew with Your wind, the sea covered them; they sank like lead in the mighty waters" (v. 10).

It also refers to the trepidation that gripped the surrounding tribes when they heard of Egypt's defeat. But, out of the nineteen verses that comprise the song, as many as eight are devoted purely to praise of God, of His unique power and of His guidance of Israel's destiny.

This is how one defines a Chosen People, or, more accurately, "a choosing people," because God did not choose our people until they had made their choice of Him. The well-known doggerel sums it up so accurately: How odd of God to choose the Jews! But not so odd; the Jews chose God.

Israel followed here in the footsteps of its founding father, Abraham, whose name testifies to the fact that he was "the father of the multitude of peoples." His concern was not just for his own clan. His heart, mind and prayers were inclusive, not exclusive.

And these were the sentiments displayed by the Israelites at a time when they had every cause to be xenophobic and self-congratulatory. Instead, they tempered their feelings of elation. They sang a controlled song of thanksgiving, taking full cognizance of the divine miracle wrought on their behalf; and they lamented the sad necessity for the waste of human life that their deliverance necessitated, human life that transcended the consideration of whether it was Israelite or non-Israelite, gentile or Jew.

The message of this song is so relevant to our age, indeed to every age of conflict throughout history. Its eternal application is contained in its very opening words. The rabbis point out that there is a problem with the tense of the verb *Az YASHIR Mosheh,* "Then Moses and the Israelites sang [this song]." We should have expected the verb to be couched in the past tense *(Az SHAR),* not in the future form *(yashir),* since the song is a thanksgiving for a victory already achieved!

But the answer is that this is Israel's archetypal song, one that would forever reverberate from her lips in the wake of her national victories throughout history. Those generous-spirited sentiments would constitute the spirit of Israel's perennial response to the downfall of her enemies.

And this philosophy is so vital for a civilized international community requiring to heal breaches and restore harmony between erstwhile foes and combatants, so that misunderstandings and differences do not fester and become exacerbated, so that nationalism and national pride are not given greater importance and consideration than human life and world peace, and so that religious and ethnic groups do not adopt attitudes of exclusivism that delegitimize the human rights and negate the freedom of those outside their own fraternity.

How right were those rabbis to latch on to the significance of the future tense of that verb *yashir*. For this is a song that mankind has not yet learned to sing and Israel has not yet been allowed to sing. But we have to believe that one day we will be privileged to sing it. And in anticipation of that, we recite this *Shirah* song every day in our morning service, betokening our concern for all, even for those we are constrained to disarm and defeat.

The *Shirah* demonstrates the lack of enthusiasm we derive from military exploit and victory. But its final verse is suggestive of our confidence that our blood-stained history will ultimately lead us into an era when "the Lord shall reign for ever and ever."

18

꩜

Marital Lessons
from *Shir Hashirim*

Each of our festivals has a book of the *Tanakh* that is associated with it. The accompanying volume to Pesach is *Shir Hashirim*, the majestic and lyrical love poem of the Song of Songs.

Rabbi Akivah hailed it as *Kodesh kodashim*, "holy of holies." But how naive and "naf" its troubadour-like descriptions and chivalrous lyrics must sound to most of our young people today. They treat everything, including love, in a prosaic, matter-of-fact way, with romance identified almost exclusively with sex, and the mystery of love and courtship demystified so early in the relationship, if not at the very first encounter.

Shir Hashirim can be read at various levels. It is, indeed, an account of the ecstasy of love, to the extent that a poor shepherdess is prepared to spurn the attentions of a King Solomon, no less, with his promise of rank, fame, and fortune, and to offer her love instead to the simple lad, of lowly estate, with whom life, she knows, is destined to be hard and routine. There is surely a message being conveyed here to the daughters of our materialistic age: to search for partners with qualities of heart and soul, rather than setting one's sights, first and foremost, on a lifestyle, and then settling for the first who can make that a reality.

Two verses in the song spell the folly of such an attitude. The first states: *Im yitein ish et kol hohn beito b'ahavah, boz yavuzu• lo,* "If a man were to offer all the wealth he possessed for love (if he put it all in the wife's name!), it would be utterly scorned" (8:7). One way of interpreting this is that, from the young man' s perspective also, he is being most naïve if he imagines that, by offering a woman material security alone, he satisfies all her needs, and that he can then go and, without distraction, pursue his own career, his own leisure diversions, and his own "time with the lads;" such a man is sowing the seeds of his own and his wife's unhappiness.

And this is what the Shunnemite shepherdess wisely foresaw when King Solomon began to woo her. She realized that she would ultimately become a mere chattel of the king, competing with Solomon's thousand other diversions, all of which would leave her feeling lonely, devalued, and unloved. Her relationship with her shepherd love, on the other hand, she knew would be totally and mutually absorbing. So she expresses it in that most direct and simple affirmation:

Dodi Iiy va'ani lo, "My beloved is for me, and I am for him." We are the total canvas of each other's life; we are there at all times for each other; we are each other's total priority; we will each make any material or other sacrifice required to relieve the burden on our partner.

"I am for my beloved," says the shepherdess. I will certainly not make any unreasonable demands that might overtax his ability to provide, and that might take their toll on his peace of mind and his health. "And my beloved is for me." He does not regard me as a breeding machine or a kitchen maid. He helps around the home; he does his fair share of shouldering his family responsibilities.

Shir Hashirim is not just a song of love, because in Judaism love and marriage truly go together. It thus has a profound message for those contemplating marriage in our age when so many enter that state believing that they can get out more than they put in. It is an affirmation of the power of love, the sanctity of sexuality and a rejection of pseudo-relationships. It should be prescribed reading for all couples. And this is undoubtedly why the great sage and romantic, Rabbi Akivah, affirmed that, "If all the books of the Bible are holy, Song of Songs is holy of holies." It is a book whose message is more urgent today than in any previous age.

But *Shir Hashirim* does not just focus on marriage itself, but, primarily, on the courtship of the young people and the uninhibited expression of their love during that period of courtship. As such, it raises some very fundamental questions regarding appropriate premarital behavior.

Behavioral mores change with time, not only between different societies, but also within any given
society, due to a host of sociological factors. Thus,
certain behavior that was acceptable in Patriarchal
times, such as the marriage between two sisters, was
later proscribed in the Torah. Similarly, the free verbal
expression of passionate love was regarded as sacred
poetry in the first commonwealth period of the Israelite
monarchy, when *Shir Hashirim* was supposedly written,
but was frowned upon as morally unbecoming in the
later Talmudic period of the first century. It was for that
reason that, before those Talmudic sages could accept
the book into the Canon as sacred writ, it had to be
stripped of its literal sense, and suffer a symbolic rein-
terpretation, as an allegory on the love between God
and Israel.

But this also raises a very real issue for our modern-
Orthodox, as well as our right-wing communities. We
do not speak of young couples who have abdicated
their moral conscience and are living together before
marriage, but of those who wish to find a normal path
to happiness but who are constrained by the strict
social and religious mores of their upbringing and their
communities' perceived expectations. Many of those
standards, it has to be said, have been ratcheted up-
wards by right-wing rabbis over the past decades.

Now, we can have no quibble with raised standards
if they are vital to the morality of a younger generation;
if they conform to the rabbinic criterion for innovation,
as so clearly expressed in the maxim that we do not
impose upon a community standards that it cannot

reasonably comply with; and if their introduction is not counterproductive, and calculated to create heartache and the disintegration of family life.

The love lyrics exchanged between the *Shir Hashirim* lovers highlight the very antithetical situation to that which exists in some Orthodox circles today. Unlike Bnei Akivah of thirty years ago, for example, where the opposite sexes fraternized, did mixed Israeli dancing, and courted to find their ultimate marriage partners, while maintaining, in the main, a sense of moral responsibility, today, even in so-called modern-Orthodox circles, there is a growing regimen of separatism. A *Shidduch* culture pervades which would be fine were it not creating serious problems for the young people when they are later pitched, unprepared and inexperienced, into an arranged marriage relationship with someone they have probably only met a few times before the decision to marry was taken.

At a recent international conference of *Nefesh*, the Association of Orthodox Mental Health Professionals, this very issue was discussed. It was pointed out that rabbis are more and more being approached for detailed personal and confidential information about the parents and siblings of potential partners: whether the mother of the potential bride or groom wears a *sheitl*, a snood, or a hat on top of a snood, how well-off the parents are, where they take their holidays and where they eat, what color tablecloth they use for the Shabbat table, for how long the girl's brother went to yeshivah and how well he can learn, as well as other family traits.

I myself regularly get requests for such information, and have been horrified that so many of those parents have been more interested in the material standing and external religiosity of the other side than in the personal qualities of their child's intended partner!

Rabbi Tzvi Hersch Weinreb of Baltimore, a staunchly Orthodox Rav and psychologist (whose *shul* I visited a few years ago as Scholar-in-Residence), has bravely condemned such intrusive probing. It has the dangerous effect of prompting families in such Orthodox circles to maintain a total secrecy about any of their children's medical or psychological problems for fear that it will adversely affect their chances in the *Shidduch* market. The result is obvious: Some unsuspecting partners discover, either on their wedding night or shortly after, that their relationship is going to be bedeviled with problems with which they cannot cope. It comes as no surprise, therefore, that the *charedi* communities are not immune to the entire spectrum of domestic and moral problems, including wife beating, prostitution, AIDS, and divorce, that one encounters elsewhere.

Gary Y. Rosenblatt, writing in *The Jewish Week*, states, "In today's Orthodox world, with its accelerated emphasis on marriage, there is little room for experimentation or failure. Whereas other couples would be breaking up after, say, six months of dating, the Orthodox couple may already be married at that point and, as a result, their break-up is a divorce, with all its added consequences."

This is an issue that is rarely ventilated in public in Orthodox circles. I do not wish to suggest that there is not a significant percentage of very happy *Shidduch* marriages; I know there are. But there must also be a vast number of women who can only find their fulfillment in the steady stream of children with which they are blessed, and which constitute a form of sublimation for other unfulfilled areas of their desire or ambition.

The rising divorce rate in Orthodox circles and the often suppressed unhappiness of so many young people, saddled with partners with whom they are frequently totally incompatible—emotionally, physically, or temperamentally—can no longer be ignored, and religious leaders must muster the courage to grapple with this vital issue as a matter of great urgency.

Perhaps we need to go back to *Shir Hashirim* for guidance, with its emphasis on love as the first and foremost consideration for a marriage partnership; with its uninhibited description of desire as a heaven-blessed emotion, not something to be suppressed and ashamed of; and with its affirmation of nonchaperoned courtship as offering an exultant opportunity for the celebration of a developing romance and a mutual self-disclosure whose natural denouement would be the discovery of a soul mate with whom one might confidently look forward to a lifetime of marital bliss.

19

ॐ

The Challenge
of the Omer Period

There is a tendency to view the Omer exclusively as a two-sided coin. On the one side is depicted its original, joyful significance as the period when the farmers of ancient Judea toiled to bring in the rich harvests and gloried in the fruits of their year's labor. On the obverse side is depicted the transformation of the Omer into a period of semi-mourning for an abortive revolt against Rome under Bar-Kochba in the year 135 c.e.

In fact, however, that period had already become a sad period some 65 years earlier with the destruction of the Temple in the year 70 c.e. and the overtaking of the rich farmlands of Judea by the conquering armies. The wealthy Sadducean landowners lost their estates, and all their managers and workers were slaughtered or sold into slavery.

So, already, the original joyful spirit that had characterized the months of Nisan to Sivan in Temple times, with the ripening and ingathering of the cereal crops and their consecration as a thanksgiving meal-offering in the Temple, had all been hauntingly stilled decades earlier. The abortive Bar-Kochba revolt simply put the final seal upon the end of any effective Jewish resistance, with the devastation of Judea and the execution of nearly all the leading rabbis of the generation, known as the Yavneh School, for having supported the revolt. This, in turn, was followed by a shift of the Jewish center to the Galilee, which had largely avoided the devastation of the south.

The Talmudic description of the origin of the Omer period as one of semi-mourning is significantly vague. It is a tapestry of statements by different sages, not a unified historical tradition. The first statement relates that "Rabbi Akivah had 24,000 disciples, from Gevat (in the Jezreel valley) to Antipatris (near Petach Tikvah), who all died at the same period of the year because they did not treat each other with respect."[1] This is clearly a rationale that hides more than it reveals.

The next statement, whose authorship the Talmud is unclear about, states rather cryptically, "they all died a terrible death."[2] The nature of their death is clarified by a subsequent statement in the name of R. Yochanan, that it was *askera*, croup. Now, I am given to understand that croup primarily affects young children, a fact mentioned elsewhere in the Talmud itself.[3] Furthermore, croup is hardly a contagious disease that could have caused such a large-scale decimation. Even if we assume that the translators have got the condition wrong, and that the reference here to *askera* should be redefined as a similar respiratory condition affecting adults, yet it is still difficult to imagine any disease that could have affected students living so spread out over the country, as the Talmud itself states it, "from Gevat to Antipatris." Furthermore, it is highly improbable that any disease would have been restricted to Talmudic students and not to the rest of the population. Yet the Talmud is insistent that it was only Akivah's disciples who were affected.

However, it is clear, not only from the medical improbability, but primarily from the fact that Akivah hailed Bar-Kochba, the leader of the Jewish revolt, as the Messianic deliverer, that the real facts of the situation have been suppressed, and that his pupils more than likely died in battle, fighting a revolt that their teacher had instigated.

There is a hint of this in the fact that his disciples were spread all over the country, and not in proximity to their illustrious teacher. Did they not share the sentiment of Akivah's colleague, R. Tarfon: *Akivah, kol ha-poreish mimkha k'poreish min hachayyim,* "Akivah, whoever separates from you, separates from life itself?"[4] What, then, were they doing in Gevat and Antipatris?

The two places referred to as the locations of those disciples are most revealing. Gevat, east of present day Haifa, is strategically well placed to cover the Galil, where the highest proportion of the Jewish community was living at that period. Antipatris, in Roman times, "stood at the junction of important highways leading to Jerusalem, Caesarea, and Jaffa, and is often mentioned as a military campsite"[5]

It is clear, then, that the Talmud suppressed the record of the role of Akivah in that revolt, perhaps for fear that religious leaders and their students might in future ages be targeted by our enemies as traditional fomenters of violent resistance.

Nevertheless, it has to be admitted that Akivah's was probably the most tragic miscalculation made by any rabbi throughout Jewish history. And the Talmudic explanation of the disciples' deaths—not treating each other with respect—is probably one of the greatest cover-ups of the Talmudic period!

Be that as it may, it certainly reflected a rabbinic penchant for involvement in politics, though Akivah's hawkish policy was diametrically opposed to that of previous religious leaders, such as Yochanan ben Zaccai, who succeeded, through negotiation, in winning concessions from the Romans. Akivah, however, used his unprecedented influence to promote an uncompromising nationalism, with disastrous consequences for the nation.

That whole episode should provide a timely lesson for some modern-day Israeli Rashei Yeshivah (heads of religious seminaries) who seek to rear generations of regimented disciples who will take instructions from them on every aspect of their personal, marital, business, or professional lives, teachers whom they are conditioned to believe in implicitly and follow even in matters of appropriate political opinion and affiliation, teachers who abuse the principle of *emunat chakhamim,* "belief in sages," to wield total control over a growing number of their gullible disciples.

Not satisfied with *keter Torah,* "the crown of the Jewish learning," and *keter shem tov,* "the crown of a good name," such teachers are also arrogating unto themselves *keter malkhut,* "the crown of political and temporal leadership."

The precedence of the Bar Kochba debacle: the transformation of a difficult situation for Jews and for Israel into an impossible one; the abandonment of a policy of accommodation with Rome, which might well have saved our homeland and prevented our exile and dispersion, for a policy of desperation and misplaced heroism (as affirmed by Akivah's own colleagues, who told him that "weeds will grow out of your jaws and the deliverer will still not have arrived")—All that should serve as an awesome warning to those extremists who would repeat the tragic misjudgments and policies of the past.

Already *Medinat Yisrael* has enabled us to reclaim two days of the *Omer* period—Yom HaAtzmaut and Yom Yerushalayim—as occasions for celebration. The stark choice before the religious politicians and rabbinate of Israel today is whether they are going to help us reclaim the entire calendar in such a spirit, or, God forbid, to give us further cause for lament.

Let us hope that a *ruach da'at,* a sensible spirit, will prevail, and that the momentum for religious tolerance and political moderation will win the day, so that we can all proclaim, in the words of the psalmist: *Sha'alu shelom yerushalayim yishlayu ohavayikh,* "Seek the peace of Jerusalem; may those who love her prosper." *Yehiy shalom b'cheileikh shalvah b'armenotayikh,* "May there be peace within your ramparts and prosperity in your grand places" (Psalm 122:6).

NOTES

1. Tal. *Yevamot* 62b.
2. *Loc. cit.*
3. Tal. *Taanik* 27b.
4. Tal. *Kiddushin* 66b.
5. *Encyclopaedia Judaica,* 3, p. 78.

Lag b'Omer and
World Reconciliation

Pirkei Avot contains a statement that is more extreme and life rejecting than any that might be preached today in the yeshivot of Meah She'arim. The author is R. Jacob of Korshai, a second-century sage and contemporary of the more famous R. Shimon bar Yochai. He states: *Ham'haleikh baderekh* . . . "If someone is going along the way, mentally revising his Torah studies, and he interrupts to admire the beauty of a particular tree or the planted symmetry of a particular field, Scripture regards it as if he had committed a mortal sin."[1]

This is an alarmingly extremist viewpoint that seeks to make a total separation of Torah from life, and to seal the students of Torah, like hermits or monks, inside their academies, divorced from both the temptations and the realities of life and the beauty of nature. This is a far cry from the life-affirming blessings that were composed by other talmudists for us to recite over such appearances as beautiful trees, animals, new blossoms, or the sight of a rainbow, all of which presuppose a divinely implanted sense of wonderment and appreciation of the manifold gifts of nature.

So how do we get to a situation where a sage like Jacob of Korshai could possibly recommend to his disciples that they detach themselves, not just from the legitimate pleasures of life, but from life itself, making study of Torah their sole *raison d'etre*, and dubbing any interruption, even for a glance at the divine handiwork, a mortal sin? To understand R. Jacob's position we have to appreciate the political and social climate of his time. He lived through the great war against the Romans, which culminated in the destruction of the Temple, followed by an intensification of the iron fist of Roman rule in Judea. This sparked off a further rebellion against the Emperor Trajan in 115–117 C.E., which was so widespread that it involved almost the entire Diaspora, pitting the Jews against Greek and Roman battalions in Libya, Cyrenaica, Egypt, Cyprus, and Mesopotamia. The desperate Jewish struggle against their invaders continued throughout the reign of Trajan's successor, Hadrian, and the death toll reached into millions.

This situation hardened Jewish attitudes, and thus was created a philosophy of despair, espoused by many sages, such as Rabbi Jacob of Korshai in that passage of *Pirkei Avot*. As far as they were concerned, the Jew had but one place of refuge, and that was the Bet Hamidrash, the academy of learning. Anywhere else was dangerous, soul destroying, and morally corrupting.

To think of creating plantations or expecting trees to survive the seizure and devastation of the insensitive and cruel occupying army, was, according to the view of those sages, naïve in the extreme. Why admire that which is transient, that which you will bless one day and whose passing you will lament the next? Secular life was an illusion; beauty a delusion. The only thing that partakes of permanence, that will provide intellectual pleasure and stimulation to the mind of the Jew, and enrichment to his otherwise impoverished life, is Torah. The only balm for his afflictions, the only ease for his torment, were the words of the living God. Immerse yourself in it, says R. Jacob, to the exclusion of all else.

Rabbi Jacob's exclusivist philosophy has a direct link to the festive day of Lag b'Omer, in that it links up with the political and religious orientation of R. Shimon bar Yochai, perhaps *the* arch-exponent of that anti-Roman and anti-secularist philosophy, whose name is particularly associated with the celebrations of that day.

Let me tell you of a famous episode in his life that exemplifies so dramatically that tension between Torah and worldly pursuits. It is recorded in Talmud *Shabbat* 33b:

> *It is about the year 130 C.E. and three leading scholars, Rabbi Judah bar Ilai, R. Yose, and R. Shimon bar Yochai, are sitting together. With them is a student, Judah ben Gerim. They soon got round to the familiar discussion of Roman rule in Judea.*

R. Judah casually observes: "What impressive things those Romans have introduced here: roads, marketplaces, bridges, and bathhouses."

R. Yose remains silent.

Rabbi Shimon bar Yochai is incensed. "They've only done it for their own advantage: roads and marketplaces to install harlots there; bridges to levy tolls and bathhouses to beautify their bodies."

Unknown to the colleagues, Judah ben Gerim was actually an informer in the pay of the Romans. He went and reported the incident to the authorities, who decreed that Judah, who had praised them, should be elevated; Yose, who kept silent, should be exiled; and Shimon bar Yochai, who condemned them, should be sentenced to death.

Shimon fled, taking his son, Rabbi Eliezer, with him. They hid in a cave, where God miraculously provided a carob tree and a well of water for their sustenance. They never stepped out of that cave for some twelve years, during which they were totally occupied with the study of Torah and its mystic interpretations.

On news of the death of the emperor, they emerged from the cave. Seeing the people plowing the fields and sowing seeds, they exclaimed, "These people are forsaking chayei olam, eternal values, and embracing chayei sha'ah, transient, worldly pursuits!"

Wherever they cast their eyes was immediately consumed by a tongue of fire, whereupon a heavenly voice exclaimed: "Is this why you have emerged, to destroy my world? Return to your cave!"

So they returned, and stayed there another year until they heard another heavenly voice telling them to return to the world.

It was the eve of Shabbat *when they emerged, and the first thing they saw was an old man carrying in his hand two bundles of myrtle, a sweet-smelling herb, having the perfume of paradise.*

"What are they for?" they asked the old man.

"They are in honor of Shabbat," *the old man replied.*

"Behold how dear God's commandments are to Israel," said Rabbi Shimon to his son.

There is, of course, a mass of cryptic meaning in this story, recounting how R. Shimon and his son graduated from exasperation and disgust with this world, which resulted in their actually trying to destroy the efforts of those fellow Jews who were engaged in constructive, worldly activities, to a position of reconciliation with it.

The old man in the story is the Jewish people, prematurely worn out, physically and emotionally, by the military and moral onslaughts of those who would subdue her. Shimon bar Yochai's flight, from the dangers of a hostile and debauched society into a self-imposed solitariness, represents the natural impulse of the pure and the godly when assailed by a permissive, godless, and violent world. One can understand the attraction of the safe, rarefied atmosphere of the Bet Hamidrash, where decisions are taken out of one's hands, where one is surrounded by gentle, kindred spirits and is cushioned from the slings and arrows of competitive and combative colleagues, and the snares of a climate of moral license, and where one's basic needs are provided without one having to worry about earning a livelihood.

But that final year in the cave, reflecting on God's censure, "Have you come to destroy my world," effected a major reassessment of Shimon bar Yochai's philosophy. He must have agonized over the implication of the words, "*My* world," with its overtone of a possession, a valued, even prized, possession. Shimon had to come to terms with that; he had to explore the interface between secularity and spirituality, and to analyze how precisely they might coexist and be mutually complementary, if not enriching. He had to reevaluate the relationship between *chayyei olam*, "eternal values," and *chayyei sha'ah*, transient, earthly, and secular pursuits. He had to fathom precisely how that synthesis of the two promoted and facilitated the essential unity of "*My* world."

But there was something else that changed Shimon bar Yochai's mind. It was the simple and charming sight of Israel beautifying her *Shabbat* with a posy of fragrant myrtles. Unlike his colleague, R. Jacob of Kurshai, who could not see any place for an appreciation of nature when one could be studying Torah, Shimon bar Yochai was alerted to the full implication of that emphasis on "*My* world," namely that absolutely everything can be pressed into the service of God, and that the beauty of His handiwork can be as potent a stimulus to spirituality for some as a Torah text itself.

Shimon and his son emerged from the cave on Lag b'Omer, the same day that he eventually departed this world. And hence that day is known in the mystic tradition as *Hillula deRashbi*, "the celebration of R. Shimon bar Yochai." And it is for this reason that, on Lag b'Omer thousands of religious families descend each year on Meron, near Safed, the site of his grave, where they recite prayers, light candles and bonfires, and perform *Opschiren*, the cutting, for the first time, of the hair of their 3-year-old children.

To my mind there is a supreme irony in the choice of this particular day, Lag b'Omer, for such a celebration of the emergence of Rabbi Shimon from his cave. For, as we have noted, that emergence marked Shimon's accommodation with worldly pursuits, whereas a very high proportion of those who converge on Meron these days, to celebrate his *Hillula*, have, in effect, returned to the cave, and given up on any accommodation with those who have had no exposure to the *chayyei olam*, the religious way of life and the eternal values!

Let us hope that the message of Shimon bar Yochai's conversion to a more holistic approach to spirituality and a more tolerant approach to the world and to one's fellow Jews, will be taken to heart, so that the unity that has always been our proudest boast will speedily become a reality.

NOTE

1. *Pirkei Avot* 3:9.

Index

About the Author

Rabbi Dr. Jeffrey M. Cohen has distinguished himself in the field of religious affairs as a broadcaster, lecturer, writer, and reviewer. A graduate of Jews' College, London, and the Yeshivot of Manchester and Gateshead, he gained a first class honors degree and a master's degree in philosophy from London University and a Ph.D. from Glasgow University. He is the author of fourteen books—the most recent being *Prayer and Penitence: A Commentary on the High Holy Day Machzor, Following the Synagogue Service, 1,001 Questions and Answers on Pesach, 1,001 Questions and Answers on Rosh Hashanah and Yom Kippur*, as well as over 300 articles. Rabbi Cohen currently serves as senior rabbi of the Stanmore Synagogue in London, England, the largest Orthodox congregation in Europe, and is a past member of the Chief Rabbi's cabinet. He and his wife Gloria have four children and ten grandchildren.